Persuasion: Social and Scientific Dynamics

Persuasion: Social and Scientific Dynamics

Austin Mardon
Thomas Banks
Juliana Quan
Madeline Langier.

Edited by Catherine Mardon

GM
★
PRESS

Cover Design & Typeset by Joshua Kramer

Print ISBN: 978-1-77369-834-2
eBook ISBN: 978-1-77369-835-9

Golden Meteorite Press
103 11919 82 St NW
Edmonton, AB T5B 2W3
www.goldenmeteoritepress.com

Contents

Chapter 1: Introduction

Persuasion has endured as an area of philosophic and public appeal for thousands of years. The elements of persuasion were defined by Aristotle in his treatise on the subject, Rhetoric, written in the 4th century BCE. Aristotle set out that the practice of persuasion is composed of the speaker's character as perceived by the audience (ethos), the audience's emotional response to the speaker (pathos), and the intrinsic rationality or soundness of the speaker's arguments (logos) (Triadafilopoulos, 1999, p. 745). As readers will see, Aristotle's ancient analysis of persuasion continues to have relevance in the modern study and practice of persuasion. For clarity, however, this book focuses not on Aristotelian persuasion but rather on persuasion as a distinct concept of modern psychology. In particular, this book operates on the definition of persuasion as the expression of "human communication designed to influence the autonomous judgments and actions of others. Persuasion is a form of attempted influence in the sense that it seeks to alter the way others think, feel, or act, but it differs from other forms of influence." (Jones & Simons, 2017, p.7). In this way, persuasion is different from coercion (threatening a sanction unless someone complies) or inducement (offering an incentive for compliance). Indeed, although they are interrelated, persuasion is different from manipulation as the intent behind a persuasive message is to enable the target audience to subjectively uncover the truth as opposed, in the case of manipulation, to the negative intent to deprive an individual of their rational agency through obfuscation. This book draws out the social and scientific dynamics of persuasion in its classical and well-meaning form.

This book aims to offer readers guidance and information on the theory, practice, and usage of persuasion as a companion of influence and power. Readers should care about the content of this book because persuasion is a foundational skill in life. Indeed, it has been concluded by economists that a quarter of the gross domestic product (the measure indicating the size of an economy) of the United States of America is based on the application of persuasion (McCloskey & Klamer, 1995, p. 191). Persuasion is a capacity that is constantly utilized and refined as individuals try and convince friends, acquaintances, and strangers to believe certain facts, to take particular action, or to reveal information. Persuasion is used in sales and marketing, in meeting and learning more about new people, in leadership, in personal relationships, and in employment and corporate contexts. It can be used in negotiating for a salary raise, bargaining for the purchase of a car, or in explaining one's political view. Likewise, persuasion is bound up in serious and fundamental aspects of society like law and order. The opportunity to persuade is at the heart of the natural justice tradition that is represented within the Western legal order which emphasizes the right to a fair trial, the opportunity to have legal representation, and the right for an accused to address allegations made against them as in Canada's Charter of Rights and Freedoms. And beyond possessing the ability to deploy persuasion effectively, it is important to be able to recognize and respond to persuasive messages and thus become a more free and independent thinker. Persuasion is essential to life in the modern world where there is an information flow that is fast and sophisticated actors are constantly using persuasive messaging to drive economic activity and political movement. Readers should pay attention to this content because understanding the fundamentals and practice of persuasion gives individuals more control and freedom in their everyday lives.

The use of persuasion requires a deep knowledge of motivation, psychology, empathy, sympathy, and human intellectual and emotional drives. Therefore, this book aims to bring together a wide variety of perspectives and academic reviews on the subject of how persuasion operates. In Chapter 2, we review a variety of practical techniques and persuasive principles individuals can use in their everyday lives. In Chapter 3, we discuss several models for understanding leadership and extrapolate from these theories recommendations for persuasive communication. In Chapter 4, we discuss social bargaining and human motivations from the perspective of mathematically modelling the persuasive choices individuals make in the context of collaboration, competition, and negotiation. In Chapter 5, we discuss the psychological foundations of persuasion and offer practical tips for increasing the effectiveness of one's persuasive message with a case study. In Chapter 6, we discuss the challenges, opportunities, and processes of the highest-staked persuasion between individuals occurring in the domain of global law and international systems. In Chapter 7, we analyze the application of persuasion in a consumer, retail, and marketing perspective drawing on the theory of cognitive psychology, self-control, and conformity. In Chapter 8, we address the means by which powerful forces exert influence over individual behaviour and, therefore, culture as a means to serve particular ends in the present and in the past using techniques of propaganda and persuasion. In Chapter 9, we analyse the forms of persuasion underlying the creation and development of conspiracy theories, social crises, and celebrity from the past to the present.

References

Jones, J. G., & Simons, H. W. (2017). *Persuasion in society.* Routledge.

McCloskey, D., & Klamer, A. (1995). One quarter of GDP is persuasion. *The American Economic Review, 85*(2), 191-195.

Triadafilopoulos, T. (1999). Politics, Speech, and the Art of Persuasion: Toward an Aristotelian Conception of the Public Sphere. *The Journal of Politics, 61*(3), 741–757. https://doi.org/10.2307/2647826

Chapter 2: Persuasive Technique

"Rhetoric is the art of ruling the minds of men."

- Plato

The process of persuasion can be described as the conscious effort of linking in a chain of argumentation separate contributions in a sequence so as to move the target audience forward toward the end conclusion and overcome the tendency of human psychology for inaction or habitual action (Stanchi, 2006). The purpose of this chapter is to review the tools, techniques, and practices that can be applied by an individual in the course of conversation and social engagement with the target audience that will increase the persuasive power of their messages. Prior to reviewing persuasive strategies, however, it is important to understand the contextual background for how persuasion occurs. The leading scientific framework for understanding persuasion is the Elaboration Likelihood Model which is based on the view that a given target audience's level of motivation to perceive the message and their intellectual ability to receive the message will determine their "elaboration likelihood" and, in turn, will impact the method of persuasion that is best suited to effect their perspective (Stanchi). The effectiveness of persuasive messages has been most often investigated in terms of rational (fact-based) and emotional (attempts to elicit certain experiences). However, there is no clear method for separating them and this chapter will review persuasion holistically.

In order to develop a message that a target audience has motivation to hear requires knowledge of and attention to the message's personal relevance to the target, the need for the target to undertake mental effort in perceiving the message, the target's perception of the source of the persuasion, and whether the message communicated accords or breaks from the target's view (J. Kitchen et al., 2014 at 2035). The target's intellectual ability to process the message is mediated by the presence of distractions, the number of times the message is repeated, the prior experience of the target, and the amount of background knowledge and experience they have (2035). If the target has a high response on these indica, then their interpretation of the message will occur via the central route and will be more lasting compared to if they are low and interpretation occurs on the peripheral route which requires little cognitive effort and more on mental shortcuts. While processing can occur in both pathways, it is ideal to achieve persuasion via the central route in order to maximize the effect of persuasion (2039). However, the peripheral route is advantageous as it is impacted subconsciously by fixed action patterns, such as the urge to look at what someone is pointing at, which are biologically established (Levine, n.d). To impact information processing within the mind of a target audience and increase acceptance of the persuasive message, there are six fundamental aspects of human behaviour that have key impacts on whether or not the persuader can elicit in the target an acceptance of their proposition. These aspects have been defined as consistency, likability, authority, reciprocity, and scarcity (Cialdini, 2001). However, other methods and techniques adjacent to these key areas will also be discussed. In what follows, this section addresses the principle, proof, and practicality of different types of persuasion based on these key aspects of human psychology.

Consistency

To use consistency in persuasion, the persuader must secure from the target audience a public or verbal pronouncement of their agreement or commitment to a persuasive message rather than merely relying on issuing an ask or command. The psychological principle underlying this form of persuasion is that the target audience is more likely to remain committed to their agreement to the pervasive message when their commitment is publicly expressed (Hollenbeck et al., 1989). Public commitments to persuasive messages are more powerful than private commitments given that there is potential for damage to reputation as a result of non-fulfilment and, moreover, that public expressions integrate themselves within one's self identity. This tool of persuasion depends upon the inherent preference individuals have for self-consistency (behaving as one states they will behave) that likely arises as a result of evolution but, moreover, exists as a personality trait in many people (Gopinath & Nyer, 2009, p. 61). This method of persuasion has a limitation in that its effectiveness depends on an individual's belief in trait or personal characteristic stability over time (Rhoads & Cialdini, 2002). The success of this method of persuasion depends on aspects of human psychology that gear a target audience to be avoiding making decisions that are inconsistent with past decisions and making decisions that express one's conception of the self or ego (Stanchi, p. 420). Moreover, another psychological factor mediating the effectiveness of consistency persuasion is the extent to which the target audience of the persuasion has susceptibility to normative influence. This susceptibility is defined as the extent to which an individual is likely to act for the purpose of identifying with others to enhance their own image as perceived by others, such as by purchasing products to fit in (Wooten & Reed II, 2004).

Moreover, the foot in the door method of persuasion relies on consistency because it depends on the target audience acceding to one request means that acceding to a later request would likewise be consistent. This technique of persuasion involves the persuader making a small request of the target audience that is likely to be accepted and then following this request with a larger request. As a matter of practicality, research indicates that applying this method requires moderating the demands of each of the requests properly (so the first request is challenging yet highly achievable), allowing the person to fully complete the first request, offering positive support and labelling the target audience as a supporter/helpful, and making the second intended request similar to some degree to the initial request (Burger et al., 2004. p. 323). This method of persuasion has several risks which must be avoided by the persuader. For instance, this method will be undermined if the persuader fails to get persons to agree to the initial request, attempts to deliver the second request for something different immediately after, or offers an incentive to the first request such as monetary remuneration or a favour (323). In addition, to the foot in the door method of persuasion, there is a related persuasive strategy referred to as the door in the face method. This persuasive strategy can be characterized by a persuader making a large request immediately to the target audience with the intent that the request will be denied. The persuader then makes to the target audience a smaller request which is presented to seem reasonable in light of the dramatic first request (Stanchi, p. 427). These methods of constancy persuasion are both effective. However, evidence concerning which of the two methods are more effective is uncertain and it is likely situationally dependent (Rodafinos et al., 2005, p. 238). Overall, persuaders should aim to use these consistency persuasion techniques on persons with traits preferences for constancy and susceptibility to normative influence. And, in order to apply consistency in persuasion practically, it is advisable to secure public commitments in conditions where the persons perceiving the commitment are of high importance to the target (Gopinath & Nyer, p. 555).

Likability

To use likability in persuasion, the persuader must convince the target audience of their goodness and friendliness. The psychological principle underlying this form of persuasion is that being dislikable is a negative affect that will reduce the good-will the target audience has for the persuader. As proof for this proposition, a study reviewing juror perceptions of expert witnesses found that "less likeable experts were considered less persuasive than more likeable experts, irrespective of evidence quality" (Younan & Martire, 2021, p. 11). This study demonstrates the importance of likability to increase persuasion endures even in contexts where the persuader has full technical experience over the subject at issue. Evidence indicates that among these forms of persuasion, liking and reciprocity are most commonly used in an interview setting in order for the persuader to build rapport with the target (Goodman-Delahunty & Howes, 2014, p. 270). In particular, this study found that "humour, informality, similarity and dissimilarity were all important" in the efforts taken by candidates to persuade the target audience to hire them (284). There are several techniques which a persuader can use in order to enhance their liveability from the perspective of the target audience.

First, a persuader can work to increase the perceived similarity between them and the target audience. People with similar backgrounds, belief systems, and experiences select to be more friendly and accepting with each other. Evidence indicates that it is possible to enhance one's influence and connection to others by finding "genuine common interests and by establishing good will and trust" (Hoy & Smith, 2007, p. 159). This can be achieved by a persuader via matching the contributions of the target audience, developing colleagueship and horizontal support concerning your influence as people imitate the behaviours of those they are similar toward, demonstrating experience in order to establish credibility in a given area, building and establishing trust by providing confidential information, and working to develop a sense of self efficacy because a firm belief in one's skills, capacities, and abilities enables one to perform better in health, academic, and fitness dimensions, and being purposefully optimistic as it counteracts learned pessimism (159-164). Similarity can also be drawn in reference to one's clothing style, interests, hobbies, and life background. Persuasion based on similarity has been tested in the context of the sharing of incidental commonalities like a birthday, first name, clothing or an interest are potential ways for a persuader to unlock in the target a "I say yes to people like this" heuristic and thus increase compliance and acceptance of their message (Burger et al., 2004, p. 42). This method of persuasion is often used in advertising and celebrity endorsement when a company trades on the goodwill, appeal, and similarity a popular individual has in order to enhance uptake of their brand (Cialdini 2009, 163). Overall, it is advisable as the persuader to appear as similar as possible to the target. Similarity has been found to increase the target's attraction, trust, and understanding for the persuader's messages (Martensen et al., 2018, p. 338).

Second, another route to achieving a likeability-persuasive advantage is to be more attractive to the target audience. The evolutionary basis for the bias toward attractive persuaders is based on that it is assumed that there is positive selection in mate selection insofar as high status intelligent persons are assumed to be more correct (Vogel et al., 2010), p. 840). Evidence confirms that physical attractiveness ratings independently predict the expectation of persuader success on targets that have low inclination for cognitive effort (840). Facial fat is a predictor of attractiveness and leadership ability. Those with more moderate or slim faces are rated as being more attractive and better leaders (Re & Perrett, 2014, p. 683). Moreover, persuasion may be impacted by the extent to which a persuader is seen by the target audience as dominant. Evidence indicates that some faces are perceived as more dominant while others are perceived as more submissive. Research shows that individuals with faces that are rated as more dominant are more likely to secure high ultimate rank within the United States military than individuals without these features (Mueller & Mazur, 1996, p. 823). This effect has also been observed in beauty in politics. One study reviewing the effect of attractiveness in Finnish political andantes, a career defined by persuasion and communication, concluded that an "increase in beauty of one standard deviation is associated with a 20% increase in the number of votes" (Berggren et al., 2010, p. 15). Research has found several hacks that individuals may be able to increase their perceived attractiveness and thus increase one's persuasive influence. For example, it has been suggested that wearing sunglasses may increase facial symmetry and therefore increase facial attractiveness (Graham & Ritchie, 2019, p. 462). Moreover, a study reviewing color and attractiveness concluded that "women perceive men to be more attractive and sexually desirable when seen on a red background and in red clothing" but that this effect does not exist for men in regard to women (Elliot et al., 2010, p. 399). Other research indicates that increasing the definition of secondary sex characteristics (pitch of voice, the chiselled jaw, coloration) can lead to increased ratings of attractiveness (Little et al., 2011, p. 1642). Overall, it is possible for individuals to increase their persuasiveness by increasing their attractiveness.

Third, it is possible to be more likeable by being more pleasant. For instance, it is advisable to offer specific, genuine and pleasing compliments and pursue flattery which leaves the target audience in a more positive mood (Vonk, 2002, p. 525). The persuasive effect of complimenting a target audience is so powerful that it endures even in cases where the target audience is aware that the persuader has alternative motives for the compliment and mentally corrects the validity of the compliment (Chan & Sengupta, 2010, 131). And, more broadly than engagement by flattery, it is advisable in the context of persuasion to engage the target audience in a way that captures their attention and relates to their personal attributes such as their background, worldview, and values (Stanchi, p. 25). For example, this can be done by drawing parallels between the target audience and a cause or person for which a persuader is attempting to inspire sympathy (Stanchi, p. 449). Overall, being a likeable and engaging speaker will increase the persuasive power of a communication.

Authority

To use authority, a persuader can leverage institutional or symbolic credibility in order to increase the extent to which the target audience is prepared to accept their message. The basis for authority is that there is a person or organization of high social status which is generally agreed to have some level of earned control. Authority is also present in the coercive power of a person integrated in a system that can offer sanctions (Searing, 1995, p. 690). Persuasion based on authority is effective because there is a long-established social leadership heuristic that demands that individuals with little expertise and background rely on the advice of those that know better (Searing, 681). However, it is important to clarify that in the context of persuasion authority is not the same as power. Power produces an obedience that is based on dealing out punishments and presenting incentives gifts. Authority, by contrast, is based on the obedience held as a result of respect. While persons in authority often have the ability to offer within an organized and sanctioned framework incentives and patronage, this is not the basis of their persuasive ability (Searing). Authority is persuasive because it often leverages the higher credibility of institutions. For instance, a degree from Harvard Medical School increases the authority of the holder because of the credibility of the institution. Evidence reviewed shows that in almost all cases "high-credibility source is more persuasive than is a low-credibility source in both changing attitudes and gaining behavioural compliance" (Pornpitakpan,

2004, p. 266). Moreover, evidence indicates that source credibility with political figures will enhance whether an individual adopts a particular policy issue (Madsen, 2016, p. 5). Authority increases credibility which, in turn, increases persuasiveness.

Authority is perhaps the most powerful persuasive tool that is possible to utilize. As evidence for the persuasiveness of authority is that it can compel ordinary persons to do otherwise unthinkable acts. The leading example of the power of authority is a series of experiments carried out in the 1960's by Stanley Milgram in which student participants administered electric shocks of gradually increasing voltages to a subject whom they believed was real at the request of a supervising scientist. Remarkably, a high proportion of participants up to 65% (n = 40) administered what they believed to be a fatal level of electricity despite hearing screams of protest and anguish which they believed were real (Slater et al., 2006, p. 1). The chilling persuasiveness of authority is clearly expressed in the diary of Milgram, writing: "I observed a mature and initially poised businessman enter the laboratory smiling and confident. Within 20 minutes he was reduced to a twitching, stuttering wreck, who was rapidly approaching a point of nervous collapse. He constantly pulled on his earlobe and twisted his hands. At one point he pushed his fist into his forehead and muttered: "God, let's stop it." And yet he continued to respond to every word of the experimenter and obeyed to the end. (Milgram, 1963, p. 377)." Authority is persuasive because it can enable a target audience to experience a diffusion and displacement of responsibility in that their ownership over situations or ideas is suppressed and they are more willing to do as instructed (Bandura, 2011, p. 3). However, it is important to note that authority is limited as a persuasive strategy because its staying power is dependent on the extent to which the perceiver believes it is valid. The persuasive basis for authority is that the target audience must perceive it as beneficial to society and the values of the target, that the authority is fair and impartial in its application of costs and rules, and that there is a generalized belief in the legitimacy of the authority (Bickman, 1974, p.58). Therefore, individuals using persuasion based on authority must ensure to maintain these principles or otherwise risk undermining their cause.

From a practical perspective, authority can be expressed to the target audience by clothing and symbols in order to strengthen the persuasive value of a message. This aspect of authority persuasion was confirmed in an experiment that assessed the level of compliance among random individuals in public with demands from a security guard. The study confirmed that the guard uniform increased compliance for mild demands (eg. giving change to a person in need) significantly and that the compliance effect did not require the constant presence of the guard (Bickman). Likewise, the persuasive effect of authority was observed in a study that showed that individuals were significantly more likely to break the law if they observed such actions from a person in a pressed suit compared to one in standard casual clothing (Cialdini, 2014, p. 189). These studies indicate that individuals intending to persuade the target should attempt to leverage their connection to authority in the communication of their messages or establish their underlying credibility, especially in their appearance and presentation to the target audience. Related to authority is the idea of social status, or the perceived position that an individual holds within the social hierarchy, based on education, income, and occupation as defined by the American Psychological Association. Authority and status are closely interrelated as persons in power are often those with authority and vice versa. Persons with high social status are given greater deference and more room for error compared to those with low social status. This effect of social status was observed in a study reviewing the behaviour of drivers and found that drivers are less likely to honk a high-status cars blocking an intersection and that the likelihood of a car to honk increases monotonically with the prestige of the car (Jann & Coutts, 2017, p. 19). This research indicates that consumer markers of social status have the potential to give the persuader a greater forgiveness, deference, and acceptance of their actions and message from the perspective of the target audience. In practice, consequently, it is reasonable to conclude that persuaders should display and enhance their social status before their targets as a result of acquiring and displaying luxury and rarefied items in addition to having an affiliation to an institution or group with credibility.

Reciprocity

To use reciprocation in persuasion, the persuader must give something over or accede to a request from the target audience. The principle underlying this form of persuasion is that the target is more favourable to persuasion when they believe that there is an ongoing exchange for mutual benefit and that the persuader is receptive to their perspective and contributions. This principle was confirmed in a study which found that targets are more likely to agree and change their perspective on a topic when their persuader earlier yielded to one of their arguments or persuasive attempts and, inversely, that uncompromising persuaders that gave no ground were less successful (Cialdini et al, 1992). In order to apply reciprocation in persuasion to maximal benefit, it is important for persuaders to recognize the issues on which it is possible to make concessions or yield with minimal costs in order to reap the rewards of reciprocation on the issues of key strategic purpose. It would be self-defeating to accede to the very issue which a persuader intends on winning with the target audience. Reciprocity can be a powerful effect. In one study, it was found that a reward (a chocolate snack) induced 38.6% of interviewed participants to reveal their password to the interviewer, who was a perfect stranger, within two minutes (Happ et al., 2016, p. 376). For practical purposes, this effect can be triggered in giving gifts, free samples, or especially in doing someone a favour. In fact, evidence shows that asking for a favour is a viable strategy not only for increasing liking but also for maintaining, strengthening, and creating new relationships when the person has the ability to offer help (Niiya, 2015, p. 219). The reason for this increase in liking could be because the target sees that the persuader overcomes the concerns that asking for the favour would result in rejection or that or because asking for help concerns the persuader because it indicates their lack of knowledge and ability in some domain (Niiya, 217). Overall, reciprocation can be deployed by asking for help, giving gifts, and acceding to non-core arguments that are related to the persuasive intent of the speaker.

Reciprocity can occur in body language in addition to verbal communication. Evidence confirms that nonverbal mirroring of social cues in a group setting, by imitating posture, leg position, and face rubs, increases target perceptions of the persuasiveness of the speaker (van Swol, 2003, p. 475). In addition, persuasion can be developed psychologically via the surrounding stimuli that the persuader curates while delivering the message. In a sense, the environment reciprocates the persuasive message. This form of persuasion relies on the psychological linking of concepts which was established famously by Ivan Pavlov. In his animal experiments, Pavlov showed that he could get dogs to salivate at the sound of a bell if he conditioned them by giving them food on many occasions beforehand while ringing the bell. The two concepts, food and the bell, had become psychologically co-mingled. This theory can be applied to persuasion in the case of humans as well. For example, persuasion often occurs over the course of an enjoyable meal so that the persuasive message and the pleasure of food are linked for the target audience. This principle was established as effective in a study that found tourism websites that were designed to increase user enjoyment lead to increased engagement on the platform (Aryanto et al., 2019, p. 464).

Lastly, a persuasion technique known as the 'that's-not-all' method uses reciprocity to an extent. This form of persuasion makes the target audience believe that the persuader is being especially reciprocal by offering a deal to the target and then further sweetening the deal before the target audience has a chance to respond (Lee et al., 2019, p. 25). The theory behind this form of persuasion is that the initial persuasive message is the anchor and the target is pleased with the apparent movement of the persuader to their favour. Classically, this form of persuasion has been studied in the context of the pricing and sale of goods that offer an initial price and then an additional discount (26).

However, the underlying logic and theory applies equally to the communication of persuasive messages. The risk of using this form of persuasion is that the initial request is unreasonable leading to a negative response in the target despite the second, more favourable request (26).

Scarcity

To use scarcity in persuasion, the persuader must demonstrate that the information or message is only actionable for a certain period of time. This method is based on the inherent psychological drive that individuals have to avert losses more than to secure gains because imagining losses triggers stronger emotional reactions compared to imagining gains (Cialdini, 2004, p. 200). Evidence for this psychological principle exists in that individuals experience myopic loss aversion which states that individuals engaging in the stock market that check on their portfolio more often are more likely to sell or, in contra positive, "longer evaluation period makes a risky option with positive expected return look more attractive" (Gneezy & Potters, 1997, p. 640). And, moreover, the mere fact that something is being made scarce increases interest in it. Cidandi describes how, for instance, government censorship can have a counterintuitive effect by increasing interest and favorability to information. Furthermore, the mere knowledge that information is subject to censorship could lead the persuasion target to receive the restricted message with greater favorability as one wants what they cannot grasp. In practice, this theory indicates that persuaders should contain in their message, either implicitly or explicitly, that the information is scarce and is time sensitive so the target should act on it immediately. Moreover, persuaders should indicate that there is some effort to suppress, silence, or censor the message. In short, people put a premium on information that is scarce and persuasive messages should draw on this.

General Tips

Although much of the foregoing content has focused on the technique of persuasion in reference to consistency, likability, authority, reciprocity, and scarcity as defined by Cidandi, there are a variety of general tips applicable to persuasion efforts. For example, a persuader can strike at the human need for the acceptance of their peers and communities and leverage social validation in their message. It is commonly accepted that if a large majority of persons appear to be taking an action, then the action has some inherent sensibility to it. Conformity is persuasive. For example, one study showed that individuals will select a clearly incorrect answer to a test question when they are aware that others have all selected the incorrect answer (Larsen, 1974, p. 303). Interestingly, the persuasive effects of social conformity do not work or have a weaker effect in environments where people are anonymous (Guadagno et al., 2013, p. 58). Persuaders can increase adoption to their message by showing others similarly accept it.

The ability to influence individuals can also be achieved through simple changes in how a message is expressed. In particular, what matters is whether reasons for the persuasive effort are communicated by the persuader to the target audience. For instance, a study found that the communication of an empty justification performs with the similar level of effectiveness as a justification with valid content as compared with a mere request without any accompanying reasons (Savransky Durán, 2011, p. 5). In essence, the use of the word 'because' in a sentence is important in persuasion whether or not the content of the message that follows the word 'because' is persuasive or empty. In practice, persuaders should back requests with actual reasons or, in the alternative, with empty reasons such as "I have to cut in line because I need to get to the front".

Other research optimizing the communication of persuasive messages concerns the complexity of persuasive messages. This research indicates that persuaders should attempt to marshal as many arguments as possible in support of their position as doing so increases their perceived competence from the perspective of the target audience (6). The intent behind this form of persuasion is to bring the target closer to the story so that they have a second hand experience from the persuader (6). Furthermore, evidence concerning the ordering of arguments within a persuasive message does not confirm whether it is best or lead with the weakest or strongest arguments (6). However, research advises that for short messages it is best for the arguments to be presented from strongest to weakest while for long arguments the reverse order of the arguments is best (6). Another obvious but significant method of persuasion is simply repeating information with subtle reconfigurations and amendments so as to prevent rejection and boredom from the target (6).

Additionally, the complexity of a message can have significant bearing on its persuasive effect. Target audiences spend more intellectual effort evaluating the claims of parts of a persuasive message that portrayed as a contribution of the persuader and less on the components of the message that the persuader relates to or assumes by implication or presupposes (Vallauri, 2022, p. 301). This subtle form of persuasion trades on the fact that the target audience believes that the implied conclusion is accepted and so need only recall it and not evaluate it as new information (301). Evidence shows that there is a psychological resistance to challenging presuppositions as the target must object to the manner in which the persuader framed their message (303) and so it is conventional to accept stated presuppositions which are received in a more shallow and less assessed fashion. It is intellectually and emotionally challenging to constantly challenge presuppositions. As a result, they can be used to develop conclusions in a target audience that are subject to less scrutiny and therefore are less liable to be rejected.

Another productive approach to persuasion is to inspire and use emotions to impact reasoning in the target audience. For instance, evidence indicates that the content of an argument is more powerful if it relates to the target's hierarchy of needs or psychological drivers. Abraham Maslow developed a tiering system of needs wherein individual motivations are expressed within a hierarchy where necessities like shelter, nourishment, and security are the primary drivers, social needs and acceptance exist in the next layer, and in the final layer psychological needs of fulfilment and self actualization (Danciu, 2014, p. 20). Persuasive messages targeted at needs located lower on the hierarchy are likely to produce more dramatic responses and acceptance. Emotions come in many varieties. However, anger and fear are often used in persuasion and negotiation. Evidence reviewed indicates that it is unproductive for the purpose of negotiation to attack the opponent. Skilled negotiators allocate more time to clarifying and seeking

CHAPTER 2: PERSUASIVE TECHNIQUE

information then attacking or defending an argument (Sheppard, 2020, p. 48). Nevertheless, the strategic expression of anger as part of the negotiation process can result in the target making greater concessions. The reason for this is that the expression of anger as part of persuasion indicates that the party is near to walking away or reaching an impasse and drawing down the negotiation (Sinaceur et al., 2011, p. 1019). However, evidence reviewed indicates that threats are more effective at inspiring a change in the negotiating party than anger, in particular when they are presented in a matter of fact style or merely as a statement as to an indication of what is likely to occur from the negotiation (Sinaceur, p. 1029). Overall, persuasion can be impactful when tuned to the emotions and motivations of the target audience.

Finally, this chapter will address the persuasion strategies involved in the effort of delivering bad news. Delivering negative information that the audience may not want to hear is a frequent occurrence for persons in all areas of life. The issue with this type of communication is that sometimes the 'messenger' can be perceived less favourably as a result of providing the negative news as the target audience retaliates against it. This type of communication is especially important as research confirms that bad news is five times more impactful than good news to a relationship and is recalled for a longer duration and is often overestimated by the target audience (Bies, 2012, p. 138). Therefore, it is important to manage blame, secure one's legitimacy and influence as part of managing impressions, reduce the perceived severity of the bad news, and enable a working relationship moving forward (Bies, p. 138). The management of bad news requires a look at the preparation, delivery, and transition involved in the presentation of the information. In order to effectively deliver bad news, this research suggests prefacing your statements that you will be giving bad news, using disclaimers about why the news is bad (excuses like we were operating under time constraints), and building out a coalition of support of key persons that are already aware of the issues (Bies, p. 143). In terms of delivery, research indicates that it is best to deliver the news with interpersonal sensitivity, provide an account for the reason for the news so as to deflect blame away from the speaker delivering the information, and disclose all relevant facts without misleading the audience. Last, in terms of moving forward after the announcement, it can be useful to deflect and reassign blame to another entity in a form of scapegoating whether real or strategic (Bias, p. 148). In addition, there are some risks involved in delivering bad news effectively. By underestimating the severity of the news in order to reduce the anger response, it may blunt the needed response to the problem (Bias, p. 154). Moreover, by blaming the operating environment or a scapegoat, the lack of responsibility for the bad news may lead to repeat occurrences of the precipitating event (Bias, p. 154). Another dilemma exists in deciding whether to disclose everything or merely tell the truth but leave out some facts. In this case, the deliverer will only be protected so long as there is a highly low chance the facts are not later discovered as this leaves the audience with distrust (Bias, p. 154). In general, persuaders must tailor their delivery to the target audience receiving it and the context in which it occurs.

We have so far reviewed a variety of strategies with the purpose of increasing the effectiveness of persuaders efforts to influence the thoughts and behaviour of their targets. However, in keeping with this theme, it is likewise important to review the means by which to resist persuasion efforts. One option for this purpose is counterarguing which is the process of resisting the persuasive message directly back to the persuader. If one is impressed with their ability to resist the message with strong arguments, they are more likely to be confident in their existing perspective (Petty et al., 2014, p. 49). Another option is to purposefully generate thoughts in support of one's position without resisting messages from the persuader (Xu & Wyer, 2012, p. 920). Furthermore, it is possible to selectively process information from the persuader's messages in an effort to distort its content and render it less appealing (Cen, 2016). Source derogation is another option in which one insults or undermines the credibility and expertise of the speaker while rejecting the validity of their position (Zuwerink Jacks & Cameron, 2003, p. 146). Lastly, one can enable and allow themselves to become upset and angered by a message by using the strategy of negative affect (147). In a review of each of these methods, a study found that the most common technique of resistance was attitude bolstering, source derogation, negative affect, and selective exposure are the least popular due to the social impacts (159). Moreover, in view of these strategies, it is possible to consider how they themselves may be combatted. In particular, because counter arguing is the most effective, it is advisable to construct messages that preemptively address and neutralize the concerns that will be raised in response to an argument by a target audience. Moreover, it may be advisable to present a version of the argument by the other side that is in a weakened form in that it can appear less plausible and saddle them with the work of rebutting it and presenting their view. It is also important to spot when one is attempting to persuade.

Fallacy and Bias

In addition to classical methods of persuasion like logical appeal, character reliance, and emotion, it is also possible to advance a persuasive message by leveraging cognitive bias or subject irrationality. A persuader playing on existing cognitive biases is not necessarily acting immorally. Instead, they are rather leveraging a tool at their disposal in order to communicate effectively to a particular audience or individual. Indeed, the use of cognitive bias may even be moral and ethical for instance in the case of a charity using this type of persuasion to solicit and increase donations to support the treatment and prevention of malaria. Persuasion requires that the target engage in a degree of intellectual reasoning in order to perceive and comprehend the communication. However, individuals are not perfectly rational and reasonable and do not perceive communications in their pure form. Individuals arrange and process their thinking on mental models or schema in order to arrive quickly at more-or-less ideal decisions often in situations of uncertainty or with limited knowledge (Gigerenzer & Goldstein, 1996, p. 666). While generally advantageous, these mental shortcuts, also known as heuristics, that generally enable efficient decision making can also produce errors and failures in decision-making processes. There are a variety of these biases and their relationship to persuasion varies from case to case. In what follows, this chapter will review biases forming as a result of expert over-reliance, ad hominem, style over substance, and irrelevant thesis.

One common form of cognitive bias is to place too great a value on an expert's persuasive advice based on their credentials, communicated knowledge, or experience. Over reliance on expert advice can lead individuals to become passive and unthinking to the persuasive message communicated and, as a result, suffer harm as a result of not taking ownership and control over their situations. Expert and scientific advice has a tendency to be presented as a single definitive interpretation of the best course of action, especially in government (Stirling, 2010, p. 1029). This form of bias leads individuals and policy makers to fail to account for alternative or complementary options for solving a given set of issues. Evidence indicates that consumers who rely on expert opinions may be overly trusting and that out of pocket expenses grow in parallel to the strength of the relationship between the expert and individual (Schwartz et al., 2011, p. 173). Moreover, consumers of medical advice rarely seek second opinions to account for the potential for flawed expert views (173). This form of bias is founded on a lack of appreciation for expert fallibility and often an inability to distinguish that an expert in one area may have no expertise in another. The argument by experts is an appeal to authority without resonation that authority is often wrong. Among the most sophisticated parties, error persists. A study looking at surgeons found that a significant recent medical error was reported by 700 (8.9%) of the 7905 participating surgeons (Shanafelt et al., 2010, p. 996). This form of bias has become less evident in recent years as modern consumers of news media aggregate information and data from multiple sources and may not necessarily trust orthodox expert views on vaccines (Geiger, 2020. p. 681). However, appeals to authority continue to be one of the most common forms of argumentative fallacies.

Another form of bias which is possible to introduce in the perspective of the target audience is known as ad hominem. In this technique, the persuader attacks the person making the argument instead of the argument itself in an effort to undermine their credibility and ability to persuade. (Da & Dahlman, 2015, p. 19). This type of persuasion is illogical because the quality of a speaker's ideas is not necessarily linked to any aspect of their background or character. It can be true both that the speaker is deficient in a specific respect of their character but simultaneously correct in the present issue at hand. The application of ad hominem in persuasion often is achieved through stereotyping a given individual (21). Stereotypes are powerful labels which are widely believed to be somewhat accurate but are oversimplified. Evidence has found that targets are willing to perceive and categorize a persuader into a stereotype and then give greater credibility (Abbate et al., 2004, p. 1204). Practically, then, a persuader should take careful effort in order to utilize stereotypes and calibrate them to the specific context and message that they intend to communicate. Stereotypes are also especially useful for persons that have lower interest in processing information because they act as mental shortcuts for perceiving a person's motivation and background (1205). Stereotypes can be used to prime a target with a particular idea or expectation about what a persuader is going to say or whether their communication is credible, however the longevity of this effect is uncertain (Power et al., 1996, p. 54). An example of this form of persuasive message are communications from Donald Trump, former President of the United States, in which he used stereotypes in order to marshal support for the construction of a border wall with Mexico. Trump drew on and developed the stereotype of Mexican illegal immigrants as criminals and drug dealers in order to increase public support for protecting against an 'other' (Schubert, 2017, p. 54). However, stereotypes can also be negative to a persuader's mission. In this case, it is possible to reduce or dispel a stereotype by identifying and emphasizing common ground a persuader has with the target (Kray, 2007, p. 171). Interestingly, apart from the target of a persuasive message, stereotypes can be used internally in order to enhance the ability of the speaker. Evidence indicates that women that were emphasizing masculine traits (such as being assortative and individualistic) had greater performance in a negotiation (163). Ad hominem and stereotypes are forms of logical fallacies but have influential effects when harnessed by a persuader.

Another form of bias commonly described in the media is known as the confirmation bias. This form of bias is defined as when the target audience has a "unwitting selectivity in the acquisition and use of evidence" (Nickerson, 1998, p. 176). This form of bias is formed from the human need to treat as more favourable positive thoughts compared to negative thoughts or to discount the importance of negative facts when they turn in an unfavourable direction (197). It is also founded on that fact that people have a tendency to evaluate persuasive messages as either false or true but not often as a mix of the two (198). Another challenge is that from a psychological perspective, individuals are often accepting with a plausible explanation for an event rather than needing a deep analysis of all options (210). The concern about confirmation bias is that, given the above aspects of personality, individuals will attempt to seek evidence to reinforce their views and interpret evidence to reinforce their mistaken position. From a practical view, then, confirmation bias can be utilized by persuaders by playing up the positivity of a fact, de-emphasizing nuance, and offering explanations of events and facts that are sufficiently complex to be realistic but no go farther than achieving a mentally satisfying conclusion which can be realized by the target audience in a short period of time. Related to confirmation bias is the fallacy of the irrelevant thesis. It is often possible to link an irrelevant thesis to a conclusion which a target audience wishes to accept as a result of confirmation bias. This persuasive technique is to introduce and pursue as subject of the conversation a irrelevant or unimportant issue that is subtly different from the issue at the heart of the debate (Clements, 2013, p. 319). In summary, confirmation bias is an effective tool of persuasion when the particular perspective of a target audience is known and can therefore be reaffirmed.

Last, the fallacy known as style over substance occurs when a target audience receives a communication in a manner that dramatically impacts its persuasivenesses. Persuaders can use style over substance though several means. For example, language can be manipulated to change how the target audience perceives the message. Word choice and the expression of a persuasive message influence the extent to which the target is willing to adopt the line of reasoning. As we have reviewed, emotions influence the persuasive process. Further to this is the fact that there are particular words that are effective in persuasive messaging because of the emotional impact they have on the target audience. For instance, the word 'helps' has positive emotional associations and gives a statement the feeling of action, phrases like 'up to 30%' convey a sense of rising motion, the word 'virtually' can be used to give a sentence a false effect of power, and words like 'strengthened' employ a false sense of strength (Danciu, 2014, 26). Messages can also become more persuasive in their style based on the non-verbal physical cues of the speaker. In particular, research indicates that standing still and still, speaking at a lower pitch, standing with feet apart, and keeping gestures congruent all increase the persuasiveness and influence of the persuader (Newman et al., 2016, p. 497). Furthermore, individuals can impact their persuasion style in their physical presence. Power poses (in essence poses that take up space with open limbs) lead to the increase of the "dominance hormone testosterone, reduction of the stress hormone cortisol, and increases in behaviourally demonstrated risk tolerance and feelings of power." (Carney et al., 2010, p. 1366). These poses can be used practically by individuals engaging in the communication of a persuasive message in order to increase their feelings of confidence while speaking.

References

Abbate, C. S., Boca, S., & Bocchiaro, P. (2004). Stereotypes in Persuasive Communication: Influence Exerted by a Disapproved Source. Journal of Applied Social Psychology, 34(6), 1191–1207. https://doi. org/10.1111/j.1559-1816.2004.tb02003.x

Aryanto, R., Chang, A., & Widianto, M. H. (2019, August). Mountain Tourism Destination Website Interface Design Based on Classical Conditioning Theory of Persuasion. In 2019 International Conference on Information Management and Technology (ICIMTech) (Vol. 1, pp. 461-465). IEEE.

Bandura, A. (2011). Moral disengagement. The encyclopedia of peace psychology.

Berggren, N., Jordahl, H., & Poutvaara, P. (2010). The looks of a winner: Beauty and electoral success. Journal of Public Economics, 94(1-2), 8–15. https://doi.org/10.1016/j.jpubeco.2009.11.002

Bickman, L. (1974). The Social Power of a Uniform 1. Journal of applied social psychology, 4(1), 47-61.

Bies, R. J. (2012). The Delivery of Bad News in Organizations. Journal of Management, 39(1), 136–162. https://doi. org/10.1177/0149206312461053

Burger, J. M., Messian, N., Patel, S., del Prado, A., & Anderson, C. (2004). What a Coincidence! The Effects of Incidental Similarity on Compliance. Personality and Social Psychology Bulletin, 30(1), 35–43. https://doi.org/10.1177/0146167203258838

Carney, D. R., Cuddy, A. J. C., & Yap, A. J. (2010). Power posing: Brief nonverbal displays affect neuroendocrine levels and risk tolerance. Psychological Science, 21(10), 1363–1368. https://doi. org/10.1177/0956797610383437

Cen, Y. (2016). Understanding distortion and biases in individual information processing under social impact (Doctoral dissertation).

Chan, E., & Sengupta, J. (2010). Insincere Flattery Actually Works: A Dual Attitudes Perspective. Journal of Marketing Research, 47(1), 122–133. https://doi.org/10.1509/jmkr.47.1.122

Cialdini, R. B. (2001). The Science of Persuasion. Scientific American, 284(2), 76–81. https://doi.org/10.1038/scientificamerican0201-76

Cialdini, R. B. (2014). Influence : science and practice. Pearson Education.

Cialdini, R. B., Green, B. L., & Rusch, A. J. (1992). When tactical pronouncements of change become real change: The case of reciprocal persuasion. Journal of Personality and Social Psychology, 63(1), 30.

Clements, C. S. (2013). Perception and persuasion in legal argumentation: using informal fallacies and cognitive biases to win the war of the worlds. Brigham Young University Law Review, 2013(2), 319-362.

Da, T., & Dahlman, C. (2015). Argument types and fallacies in legal argumentation. Springer.

Danciu, V. (2014). Manipulative marketing: persuasion and manipulation of the consumer through advertising. Theoretical and Applied Economics, 21(2), 591.

Elliot, A. J., Niesta Kayser, D., Greitemeyer, T., Lichtenfeld, S., Gramzow, R. H., Maier, M. A., & Liu, H. (2010). Red, rank, and romance in women viewing men. Journal of Experimental Psychology: General, 139(3), 399–417. https://doi.org/10.1037/a0019689

Geiger, N. (2020). Do People Actually "Listen to the Experts"? A Cautionary Note on Assuming Expert Credibility and Persuasiveness on Public Health Policy Advocacy. Health Communication, 1–8. https://doi.org/10.1080/10410236.2020.1862449

Gigerenzer, G., & Goldstein, D. G. (1996). Reasoning the fast and frugal way: models of bounded rationality. Psychological review, 103(4), 650.

Gneezy, U., & Potters, J. (1997). An Experiment on Risk Taking and Evaluation Periods. The Quarterly Journal of Economics, 112(2), 631–645. https://doi.org/10.1162/003355397555217

Goodman-Delahunty, J., & Howes, L. M. (2014). Social persuasion to develop rapport in high-stakes interviews: qualitative analyses of Asian-Pacific practices. Policing and Society, 26(3), 270–290. https://doi.org/1 0.1080/10439463.2014.942848

Gopinath, M., & Nyer, P. U. (2009). The effect of public commitment on resistance to persuasion: The influence of attitude certainty, issue importance, susceptibility to normative influence, preference for consistency and source proximity. International Journal of Research in Marketing, 26(1), 60–68. https://doi.org/10.1016/j.ijresmar.2008.08.003

Graham, D. L., & Ritchie, K. L. (2019). Making a Spectacle of Yourself: The Effect of Glasses and Sunglasses on Face Perception. Perception, 48(6), 461–470. https://doi.org/10.1177/0301006619844680

Guadagno, R. E., Muscanell, N. L., Rice, L. M., & Roberts, N. (2013). Social influence online: The impact of social validation and likability on compliance. Psychology of Popular Media Culture, 2(1), 51–60. https://doi.org/10.1037/a0030592

Happ, C., Melzer, A., & Steffgen, G. (2016). Trick with treat – Reciprocity increases the willingness to communicate personal data. Computers in Human Behavior, 61, 372–377. https://doi.org/10.1016/j.chb.2016.03.026

Hollenbeck, J. R., Williams, C. R., & Klein, H. J. (1989). An empirical examination of the antecedents of commitment to difficult goals. Journal of Applied Psychology, 74(1), 18–23. https://doi.org/10.1037/0021-9010.74.1.18

Hoy, W. K., & Smith, P. A. (2007). Influence: a key to successful leadership. International Journal of Educational Management, 21(2), 158–167. https://doi.org/10.1108/09513540710729944

J. Kitchen, P., Kerr, G., E. Schultz, D., McColl, R., & Pals, H. (2014). The elaboration likelihood model: review, critique and research agenda. European Journal of Marketing, 48(11/12), 2033–2050. https://doi.org/10.1108/ejm-12-2011-0776

Jann, B., & Coutts, E. (2017). Social Status and Peer-Punishment: Findings from Two Road Traffic Field Experiments.

Kouzes, J.M. & B.Z. Posner (2007). The Leadership challenge (4th ed.). San Francisco, Jossey-Bass.

Kray, L. J. (2007). Leading through Negotiation: Harnessing the Power of Gender Stereotypes. California Management Review, 50(1), 159–173. https://doi.org/10.2307/41166421

Larsen, K. S. (1974). Conformity in the Asch Experiment. The Journal of Social Psychology, 94(2), 303–304. https://doi.org/10.1080/00224545.1974.9923224

Levine, R. V. (n.d.). 4.1.2 Persuasion: So Easily Fooled – Understanding Literacy in Our Lives. Retrieved August 14, 2022, from 4.1.2 Persuasion: So Easily Fooled – Understanding Literacy in Our Lives website: https://pressbooks.ulib.csuohio.edu/understanding-literacy-in-our-lives/chapter/4-1-2-persuasion-so-easily-fooled/

Lee, S., Moon, S.-I., & Feeley, T. H. (2019). The "that's-not-all" compliance-gaining technique: when does it work?. Social Influence, 14(2), 25–39. https://doi.org/10.1080/15534510.2019.1634146

Little, A. C., Jones, B. C., & DeBruine, L. M. (2011). Facial attractiveness: evolutionary based research. Philosophical Transactions of the Royal Society B: Biological Sciences, 366(1571), 1638-1659.

Lombardi Vallauri, E. (2022). Implicit strategies aimed at persuading the audience in public debates. Intercultural Pragmatics, 19(3), 299–319. https://doi.org/10.1515/ip-2022-3002

Madsen, J. K. (2016). Trump supported it?! A Bayesian source credibility model applied to appeals to specific American presidential candidates' opinions. In CogSci.

Martensen, A., Brockenhuus-Schack, S., & Zahid, A. L. (2018). How citizen influencers persuade their followers. Journal of Fashion Marketing and Management: An International Journal, 22(3), 335–353. https://doi.org/10.1108/jfmm-09-2017-0095

Mueller, U., & Mazur, A. (1996). Facial dominance of West Point cadets as a predictor of later military rank. Social forces, 74(3), 823-850

Newman, R., Furnham, A., Weis, L., Gee, M., Cardos, R., Lay, A., & McClelland, A. (2016). Non-Verbal Presence: How Changing Your Behaviour Can Increase Your Ratings for Persuasion, Leadership and Confidence. Psychology, 07(04), 488–499. https://doi.org/10.4236/psych.2016.74050

Nickerson, R. S. (1998). Confirmation bias: A ubiquitous phenomenon in many guises. Review of General Psychology, 2(2), 175–220. https://doi.org/10.1037/1089-2680.2.2.175

Niiya, Y. (2015). Does a Favor Request Increase Liking Toward the Requester? The Journal of Social Psychology, 156(2), 211–221. https://doi.org/10.1080/00224545.2015.1095706

Petty, R. E., Tormala, Z. L., & Rucker, D. D. (2004). Resisting persuasion by counterarguing: An attitude strength perspective.

Pornpitakpan, C. (2004). The Persuasiveness of Source Credibility: A Critical Review of Five Decades' Evidence. Journal of Applied Social Psychology, 34(2), 243–281. https://doi.org/10.1111/j.1559-1816.2004.tb02547.x

Power, G., Murphey, S., & Coover, G. (1996). Priming Prejudice
How Stereotypes and Counter-Stereotypes Influence Attribution
of Responsibility and Credibility among Ingroups and Outgroups.
Human Communication Research, 23(1), 36–58. https://doi.
org/10.1111/j.1468-2958.1996.tb00386.x

Re, D. E., & Perrett, D. I. (2014). The Effects of Facial Adiposity on
Attractiveness and Perceived Leadership Ability. Quarterly Journal of
Experimental Psychology, 67(4), 676–686. https://doi.org/10.1080/1747
0218.2013.825635

Rhoads, K. V., & Cialdini, R. B. (2002). The business of influence:
Principles that lead to success in commercial settings. The persuasion
handbook, 513-542.

Rodafinos, A., Vucevic, A., & Sideridis, G. D. (2005). The Effectiveness
of Compliance Techniques: Foot in the Door Versus Door in the
Face. The Journal of Social Psychology, 145(2), 237–240. https://doi.
org/10.3200/socp.145.2.237-240

Savransky Durán, M. (2011). "Imaginative research" on Persuasion:
Subverting apparent certainty. New Ideas in Psychology, 29(1), 1–9.
https://doi.org/10.1016/j.newideapsych.2009.10.001

Schubert, C. (2017). Constructing Mexican stereotypes: Telecinematic
discourse and Donald Trump's campaign rhetoric. Critical approaches to
discourse analysis across disciplines, 8(2), 37-57.

Schwartz, J., Luce, M. F., & Ariely, D. (2011). Are Consumers Too
Trusting? The Effects of Relationships with Expert Advisers. Journal
of Marketing Research, 48(SPL), S163–S174. https://doi.org/10.1509/
jmkr.48.spl.s163

Shanafelt, T. D., Balch, C. M., Bechamps, G., Russell, T., Dyrbye, L.,
Satele, D., ... & Freischlag, J. (2010). Burnout and medical errors among
American surgeons. Annals of surgery, 251(6), 995-1000.

Sheppard, E. (2020). Examining the characteristics and tactics of chief negotiators in Canadian universities.

Sinaceur, M., Van Kleef, G. A., Neale, M. A., Adam, H., & Haag, C. (2011). Hot or cold: is communicating anger or threats more effective in negotiation? The Journal of Applied Psychology, 96(5), 1018–1032. https://doi.org/10.1037/a0023896

Slater, M., Antley, A., Davison, A., Swapp, D., Guger, C., Barker, C., Pistrang, N., & Sanchez-Vives, M. V. (2006). A Virtual Reprise of the Stanley Milgram Obedience Experiments. PLoS ONE, 1(1), e39. https://doi.org/10.1371/journal.pone.0000039

Stanchi, K. M. (2006). The science of persuasion: an initial exploration. Michigan State Law Review, 2006(2), 411-456.

Stirling, A. (2010). Keep it complex. Nature, 468(7327), 1029-1031. van Swol, L. M. (2003). The Effects of Nonverbal Mirroring on Perceived Persuasiveness, Agreement with an Imitator, and Reciprocity in a Group Discussion. Communication Research, 30(4), 461–480. https://doi.org/10.1177/0093650203253318

Vogel, T., Kutzner, F., Fiedler, K., & Freytag, P. (2010). Exploiting Attractiveness in Persuasion: Senders' Implicit Theories About Receivers' Processing Motivation. Personality and Social Psychology Bulletin, 36(6), 830–842. https://doi.org/10.1177/0146167210371623

Vonk, R. (2002). Self-serving interpretations of flattery: Why ingratiation works. Journal of Personality and Social Psychology, 82(4), 515–526. https://doi.org/10.1037/0022-3514.82.4.515

Wooten, David B., & Reed II, A. (2004). Playing It Safe: Susceptibility to Normative Influence and Protective Self-Presentation. Journal of Consumer Research, 31(3), 551–556. https://doi.org/10.1086/425089

Xu, A. J., & Wyer, R. S. (2012). The Role of Bolstering and Counterarguing Mind-Sets in Persuasion. Journal of Consumer Research, 38(5), 920–932. https://doi.org/10.1086/661112

CHAPTER 2: PERSUASIVE TECHNIQUE

Younan, M., & Martire, K. A. (2021). Likeability and Expert Persuasion: Dislikeability Reduces the Perceived Persuasiveness of Expert Evidence. Frontiers in Psychology, 12. https://doi.org/10.3389/fpsyg.2021.785677

Zuwerink Jacks, J., & Cameron, K. A. (2003). Strategies for Resisting Persuasion. Basic and Applied Social Psychology, 25(2), 145–161. https://doi.org/10.1207/s15324834basp2502_5

Chapter 3: Persuasion and Leadership

"Leadership is the capacity to translate vision into reality."

- Warren Bennis.

Leadership is the practice of persuasion. Leadership is an interactive process that occurs between individuals in groups in which a leader affects followers via influence to achieve a shared goal or mutual purpose. Leaders have to engage in persuasion in order to be influential to their followers. Leadership, therefore, is especially about persuasion as it relates to a leader's responsibilities in establishing a vision for the future, aligning divergent interests between group members, and motivating individuals toward a common goal. Given the connection between leadership and persuasion, this chapter aims to describe and synthesise research concerning a variety of approaches to theorising about the use of persuasion in a variety of leadership styles. In particular, this chapter reviews trait-based, charismatic, skills-based, situational, goal-path, and transformational leadership styles and profiles their connection to the application of persuasion.

The trait-based theory of leadership is one conceptual framework for imagining the ideal application of persuasion. The trait-based theory of leadership is based on the idea that there are individual leaders that hold a bundle of particular traits which give them a sense of charisma or particular leadership ability. The standard and most popular psychological model for expressing personality is the Big Five Personality Trait Model. This model states that human personality can be defined in reference to the stable trait characteristics of openness, extraversion, conscientiousness, agreeableness, and neuroticism (Cobb-Clark & Schurer, 2011, p. 14). Leader emergence is best predicted by the traits consciousness and extraversion (Spark & O'Connor, 2020, p.2). Practically, this means that individuals wanting to be more persuasive and enter into a leadership position should demonstrate a high degree of confidence. Practically, according to research, confidence can be best expressed in language by "increased loudness of voice, higher pitch level (under certain conditions), shorter pauses, and a rapid rate of speech." (Scherer et al., 1973, p. 42). However, traits cannot be the only controlling factor in the leadership and persuasive ability of an individual as their context impacts their capacities. Therefore, it is important to bring other theories to bear on the issue of persuasion as a combination of them integrated in a theoretically meaningful manner is more likely to predict leadership and persuasive capacity than relying on any one theory alone.

Charismatic leadership likewise relates to persuasion and influence. Leadership scholars describe the aim of charismatic leadership as being to "increase the intrinsic value of follower efforts in pursuit of mission accomplishment by linking effort and goals to valued aspects of the follower's self-concept" (Fiol et al., 1999, 452). Certainly, readers will be aware that they meet persons that are more persuasive than others naturally or because of their character and personality. In terms of emergence, charismatic leaders often can develop in times of crisis or uncertainty where distress motivates people to perceive as qualified and follow with devotion a charismatic leader (Tucker, 2017). Charisma as a concept and expression is linked with the idea of leadership and therefore charismatic leaders have more influence (Guarana & Avolio, 2022, p. 5). The persuasive success of charismatic leaders can be traced to the manner in which they express particular values and personal identities and then integrate these factors into a framework for judging what behaviour is acceptable (Fiol, p. 453). Charismatic leadership depends on the persuasive ability of the leader to affect the self concepts of followers instead of relying on incentivization (pay) or intellectual argument. In order to achieve this persuasive aim, charismatic leadership requires the persuader to articulate an ideological vision establishing a path to a future the target believes is superior to the present, communicate moral and ethical principles, act as a role model, express high performance expectations, offer radical proposals to solve major problems, intellectually stimulate their followers, and take risks to achieve their goals (House &

Howell, 1992, p. 83). Charismatic leaders persuade in that they are confident without being aggressive and share a care and concern for their followers (90). In total, persuaders can leverage the practices of charismatic leadership in order to succeed.

The skills based theory of leadership concerns the ability of an individual to leverage their knowledge and capacities into the objective of the group. This theory is important because the extent to which an individual is able to persuade others depends on their mastery of several underlying skills. In particular, competencies like problem solving skills (using new information), social judgement (understanding people and motivations), and knowledge (understanding information generally) underlie the ability for one to persuade. These skills are often learned over time. Similarly, the behavioural theory of leadership concerns how leaders employ their skills in persuasion to affect influence. In this theory, the activities of leaders are conceptualized to either be task behaviours or leadership behaviours. In terms of leader behaviour, the Lewin, Lippett, White Study demonstrates the difference in leader styles (Scheidlinger). This research has determined that democratic leadership is the most productive on the whole and liked. Comparatively, autocratic leaders were less liked but the most productive provided that the leader was present. Laissez faire leaders are the least well regarded and the least productive. This study has three implications for persuasion. First, it demonstrates that persuasion is an active process that requires effort. Second, it establishes that persuasion is a collaborative process that depends on authority. Third, it shows that persuasion backed by the use of power is only effective when it is directly threatened. However, this model as well as those discussed previously do not consider the situational impacts of persuasion that weigh heavily on one's ability to interpret a persuasive message.

Another perspective on leadership popularized by Hersey and Blanchard indicates that the persuasive ability of a leader is mediated by their situation and context (Hersey et al., 1979). This theory describes that leaders must match their persuasive style to the context of their followers. This model classifies leader action as either directive in communicating how a task is to be fulfilled or supportive in communicating for the purpose of increasing follower appreciation (for example by commending their work, asking for their opinions, and exchanging information). This model states that followers fall somewhere on a grid of directive and supportive attributes. Individuals with high commitment and high competence need a persuasive and leadership strategy that delegates to them considerable autonomy to carry out and realize the task. Individuals with low commitment and high competence need a supportive leader that can create acceptable incentives and enable them to follow and adopt the plan. Teams with high commitment and low competence need a directive persuader that clearly establishes and commands task fulfilment. Low commitment and low competence teams require a persuader to take the position of a coach. This type of leadership and persuasion depends on leaders assessing the developmental state of their teams and having the skills to adapt to meet the needs of the team. The situational leadership model developed by Hersey and Blanchard reaffirms the importance of persuasion taking into account the unique demographics of the target audience. However, this model may not fully account for how demographic and individual differences can influence follower responses and may not recognize that each situation is highly dependent.

The path goal theory of leadership offers another framework for the application of the principles of persuasion. This theory concerns the method by which leaders motivate followers to achieve designated goals (Talal Ratyan et al., 2013). This theory states that it is the role of the leader to define goals, set a path, remove obstacles of success, and provide information to their followers. This leadership theory is based on the idea that followers are motivated because they can achieve a particular goal and that positive effects will result from such as realization. The generation of motivation requires leaders to select a style that best suits the reasonable expectations of their followers, one that communicates the greatest number of incentives that followers will receive, that clearly identifies the end goal, and that increases the personal satisfaction that targets hear from the persuasion (House, 1971). Persuasion can be used in service of each of these goals and also needs to be used to increase motivation in relative tasks. Persuasion can enable individuals to take on control in the path goal setting. For instance, in weak formal authority, persuasion needs to be used to establish command. Likewise, if the task itself is unclear, persuasion can be used to provide structure and offer guidance. However, this model is leader oriented and may fail to appreciate the extent to which persuasion is a two-way street that depends on both how the message is communicated but as well as how it is received by the target. Overall, persuaders can leverage path goal theory in order to enhance their ability to take their target audience toward their intended conclusion via the path of least resistance and challenge.

Among the different paradigms, the transformational theory of leadership has the closest relationship to persuasion. It is centred around charisma and elements of leadership. Transformational leadership is centred around the process of exchange between a leader and followers. It can be distinguished in reference to transactional leadership which is about short term exchanges and are based on self interest. In comparison, transformational leadership is about creating a connection between the persuader and the target that raises moral and motivation in a far reaching and enduring manner. Authentic leadership and its attendant persuasion are dramatic because they improve and change the moral identity and emotions of the target (Luthans & Avolio, 2003). The characteristics of charismatic transformational leaders include "expertise, trustworthiness, likeability, similarity and familiarity" which all contribute to the success of a persuader (Martensen et al., 2018, p. 447). There are several practical means by which individuals can channel transformational leadership in their own lives. According to research, the qualities involved in transformational leadership include acting as a social architect to shape the shared meanings they have with the persuasion targets and that they develop themselves in positive self regard via emphasizing their strengths and downplaying their weaknesses (Morden, 1997, p. 670). Moreover, research has identified that persuasive strategies for transformational leaders include setting an example, affirming common values, setting a clear path, being willing to challenge the status quo, rewarding people with celebrations, and building trust (Kouzes & Posner, 2007). Practically, charisma involves using metaphors, speaking about the future, setting goals, and communicating with emotions as well as being highly self-confident (believing in one's ability) and self-assured (being free of doubts) and moreover being highly persistent (pursuing goals despite challenges) and determined (acting with conviction and certainty).

References

Cobb-Clark, D. A., & Schurer, S. (2011). The Stability of Big-Five Personality Traits. SSRN Electronic Journal. https://doi.org/10.2139/ssrn.1919414

Fiol, C. M., Harris, D., & House, R. (1999). Charismatic leadership: Strategies for effecting social change. The Leadership Quarterly, 10(3), 449-482.

Hersey, P., Blanchard, K. H., & Natemeyer, W. E. (1979). Situational Leadership, Perception, and the Impact of Power. Group & Organization Studies, 4(4), 418–428. https://doi.org/10.1177/105960117900400404 House, R. J. (1971). A Path Goal Theory of Leader Effectiveness. Administrative Science Quarterly, 16(3), 321–339. https://doi.org/10.2307/2391905

House, R. J., & Howell, J. M. (1992). Personality and charismatic leadership. The Leadership Quarterly, 3(2), 81–108. https://doi.org/10.1016/1048-9843(92)90028-e

L. Guarana, C., & Avolio, B. J. (2022). Unpacking Psychological Ownership: How Transactional and Transformational Leaders Motivate Ownership. Journal of Leadership & Organizational Studies, 29(1), 96–114. https://doi.org/10.1177/15480518211066072

Luthans, F., & Avolio, B. J. (2003). Authentic leadership development. Positive organizational scholarship, 241, 258.

Martensen, A., Brockenhuus-Schack, S., & Zahid, A. L. (2018). How citizen influencers persuade their followers. Journal of Fashion Marketing and Management: An International Journal, 22(3), 335–353. https://doi.org/10.1108/jfmm-09-2017-0095

Milgram, S. (1963). Behavioral study of obedience. The Journal of abnormal and social psychology, 67(4), 371.
Morden, T. (1997). Leadership as vision. Management Decision.

Scherer, K. R., London, H., & Wolf, J. J. (1973). The voice of confidence: Paralinguistic cues and audience evaluation. Journal of Research in Personality, 7(1), 31-44.

Spark, A., & O'Connor, P. J. (2020). State extraversion and emergent leadership: Do introverts emerge as leaders when they act like extraverts? The Leadership Quarterly, 32(3), 101474. https://doi.org/10.1016/j.leaqua.2020.101474

Talal Ratyan, A., Khalaf, B., & Rasli, A. (2013). Overview of Path-Goal Leadership Theory. Jurnal Teknologi, 64(2). https://doi.org/10.11113/jt.v64.2235

Tucker, R. C. (2017). The theory of charismatic leadership. In Leadership Perspectives (pp. 499-524). Routledge.

Chapter 4: Modelling Bargaining Situations

Game theory provides an analytic framework for bargaining. It is fundamental to the understanding of persuasion, negotiation and bargaining theory and is frequently discussed in relation to economic and political theory. In this chapter the topic of bargaining and individual mechanisms of motivation that drive prosocial behaviour from a game theory perspective will be explored. The prisoner's dilemma, the Nash bargaining theory and non-cooperative bargaining theory will be introduced and then applied to various social, economic, and political situations. Many of the concepts in bargaining theory may seem intuitive, but these models are necessary to understand and provide the foundation for other more complex processes. Building off Rubenstein's (1982) model, the international relations theory, and models of war as a bargaining process will be discussed in the following chapter. Bargaining theory can help explain and predict why some actors are able to better advance their position to achieve an outcome that is more favourable to them within the bargaining range (Kim, 2018).

A bargaining situation occurs where there are two players who can mutually benefit from cooperation with a range of possible outcomes and differing interests in the possible outcomes (Muthoo, 1999).The players must reach an agreement on how to cooperate (Muthoo, 1999).Note that for the purposes of this chapter players, actors, and bargainers are used interchangeably. Both players would be better off coming to an agreement but each player wants an agreement that is most favourable to themselves (Muthoo, 1999). Real life examples have proved this task to be complex, resulting in costly delays, conflict, and failure to reach an agreement (Muthoo, 1999). Other means of reaching mutually beneficial agreements can be achieved via mediation and arbitration, however the primary focus of this chapter will be on bargaining, that is players acting on their own behalf. The greatest obstacle to effective bargaining is inefficiency (Muthoo, 1999). If there was no friction in the bargaining process, that is, costs incurred through the bargaining process, namely delay, the outcome would be indeterminate as their process would lack incentives to come to an agreement (Muthoo, 1999). Rubenstein's (1982) seminal bargaining model factored in values for time in the offer-counteroffer bargaining situation. The possibility of other external factors and their relative impact are factored into the bargaining outcome (Muthoo, 1999). Bargaining models differentiate between integrative bargaining and distributive bargaining (Kim, 2018). Where the game can be classified as a distributive bargaining situation the 'game' is a win-lose scenario where every gain to one party results in a loss to the other (Kim, 2018). These adversarial bargaining games are known as zero-sum games (Kim, 2018). More aggressive bargaining tactics, as discussed later, are typically best suited for win-lose games where there is no incentive for cooperation (Dur & Mateo, 2010). Rather, the dominant strategy is to gain as much benefit or utility as feasible (Kim, 2018). To provide a real-life example of a zero-sum game consider negotiations for the purchase of an apple. The buyer and seller engage in a negotiation dance with offers and counteroffers. In this adversarial scenario the buyer and seller try to gain as much as possible. That is, the buyer tries to gain the apple at the lowest possible cost and the seller tries to gain as much money as possible for the cost of the apple. In this scenario the assumption is a fixed pie where each player's gain is directly associated with a loss for the other party. Alternatively, an integrative bargaining scenario considers co-operation where there is the potential for a "win-win" outcome (Kim, 2018). These scenarios are referred to as positive-sum games (Kim, 2018). Three bargaining solutions will be explored in this chapter. Each of these solutions provide a formula that has a unique outcome.

The prisoner's dilemma is a classic example of bargaining and social dilemma theory and can be used to analyse bargaining in contract negotiations and international politics (Poundstone, 1993). The dominant, or best strategy, is often a valuable first step in the negotiation and persuasion strategizing (Kim, 2018). The Prisoner's Dilemma, has been applied to various real-world scenarios, including in first strike military scenarios (Poundstone, 1993). The basic premise is that individuals choose between advancing their own outcome or advancing the collective interest (Van Dijk, 2015). Each player is given the same binary option to cooperate or betray the other player (Poundstone, 1993). For both players, individually, the strategy with the greatest payoff outcome is betrayal (Kim, 2018). However, this strategy, when utilised by both players, has the worst collective payoff for the group as a whole (Kim, 2018). This economic problem, that is, the maximisation of personal gains that leads to the depletion of shared resources, is known as the *"tragedy of the commons"* (Hardin, 1968). History has shown that this problem can be a significant problem, sometimes leading to the collapse of societies (Hardin, 1968). The classic Prisoner's Dilemma game consists of multiple rounds and players are able to see their payoff after each round (Montero-Porras et al., 2022). The ideal strategy is one that results in the best payout (Turocy & Stengel, 2001). With many equilibrium outcomes possible, literature has primarily focused on strategies to encourage cooperation to optimise the collective outcome (Montero-Porras et al., 2022). The prisoner's dilemma is often described as the clash of individual and collective rationality (Eric van Dijk, 2015). In the real world there would be long-term ramifications for betrayal-betrayal strategies, sometimes referred to as mutually assured destruction in the prisoner's dilemma context (Kim, 2018). Instead of a lose-lose strategy, the dominant strategy should be one that ensures better absolute and relative payoffs (Kim, 2018). Literature indicates that the Tit-for-Tat framework, a form of the Prisoner's Dilemma strategy, may be the dominant strategy (Kim, 2018). This strategy starts with players signalling a cooperative strategy in the initial round in order to initiate a mirroring strategy (Kim, 2018). This strategy, however, may lead to non-optimal equilibrium, that is to say that there is no absolute outcome (Kim, 2018). Humans are not rational actors, and it is impossible to empirically predict, with precision, how humans will act (Kim, 2018). However, strategies such as the Tit-for-Tat framework can provide best-practice strategies that maximise persuasion success.

Reciprocity has been identified as one of the key mechanisms to support cooperative behaviour, justifying the presence of prosocial and altruistic behaviour (Cialdini, 2001). Many studies have explored the mechanisms of prosocial behaviour and reciprocity. One study introduced images of kind and unkind eyes to the classic Prisoner's Dilemma game (Pauwels et al., 2017). The data suggested that images of unkind eyes actually encouraged cooperative behaviour with the player that made the first move (Pauwels et al., 2017). The theory was that unkind eyes were a reminder of mutual beneficial behaviour and dependence (Pauwels et al., 2017). Other studies, including one that showed angry eyes have supported the idea that heightened arousal in player one supported prosocial behaviour (Gamer et al., 2010). This has been referred to as the "policing effect" (Pauwels et al., 2017). Neither image altered the behaviour of the second player (Pauwels et al., 2017). This aligns with the Tit-for-Tat framework, which predicts that the first player 'move' initiates a mirroring effect (Kim, 2018). The second player's move is dependent upon the first player's move and less prone to influence by cues of prosocial and altruistic behaviour (Kim, 2018).

Further, one cross-cultural study found that when people were reminded of their respective moralistic god, human cooperation and prosocial behaviour increased with the more punitive people rated their respective god (Purzyscki et al., 2016). Research on this "policing effect" and influence on socially desirable behaviour is inconsistent. Two meta-analyses, examining the relationship between artificial surveillance cues and generosity found there to be no behavioural effect when individuals were subjected to the policing effect of watchful eyes (Pauwels et al., 2017). Another study, that specifically examined eye cues and the effect on reciprocity, found these cues to be insignificant (Northover et al., 2016). The contrast between these studies and those that did find a correlation may be due to the experimental set up. Where, for example, in Pauwels et al. (2017) the player's relied on their beliefs about other's contributions, thus cues that signalled altruistic behaviours affected their play. Comparatively, the study in Northover et al. (2016) focused on set ups that did where there was no second player response dependent upon the first player move. The studies in the meta-analyses primarily looked at the effect of people's behaviour and fear of damage to reputation.

For example, the effect of watchful eyes and charitable donations (Northover et al., 2016). People are conditional cooperators, and their behaviour is dependent on how they believe others will act (Pauwels et al., 2017).

Negotiation and persuasion, both in theory and practice, are functions of strategy. Dominant strategies informed by relative bargaining power, alternative options to the negotiated agreement and willingness to take risks. Game theory provides a framework for negotiation strategies to increase the probability of successful outcomes. Persuasion based negotiation can be utilised to inform dominant strategies in complex real world scenarios.

The Nash Bargaining Theory is one of the most famous bargaining theories. The Nash bargaining solution and its variations have been applied to numerous scenarios from simple games such as the prisoner's dilemma to complex crises bargaining situations such as war. John Nash famously coined the Nash Bargaining Solution which provides empirical predictions for bargaining outcomes utilising an axiomatic approach (Muthoo, 1999). Essentially, there are a number of features that together, in theory, determine a unique outcome for every bargaining situation (McCarty & Meirowitz, 2007). The Nash solution provides best response strategies to other's plays (McCarty & Meirowitz, 2007). For example, in the prisoner's dilemma the best response, as discussed, is for the player to betray every time (McCarty & Meirowitz, 2007). The unique outcome for the Prisoner's Dilemma is therefore {confess, confess} (McCarty & Meirowitz, 2007). This is more complex for other games and in real-life applications (McCarty & Meirowitz, 2007). Player's aversion to risk is an important factor in bargaining situations. Players face the risk that the agreement will not be achieved. The risk that players are willing to take, depends in part on the number of other alternatives players have. One measure of this, as discussed by Kim (2018) is the Best Alternative to a Negotiated Agreement (BATNA). Where a given actor has a better BATNA and/or more options than the other player(s) we can assume that player will engage in more aggressive tactics (Kim, 2018). Players with a good BATNA have less to lose if the negotiations fail and therefore can tolerate greater risks in the negotiation process (McCarty & Meirowitz, 2007). The Nash Bargaining Model is consistent with this theory. It is implied that where one player's aversion to risk decreases the opponents risk aversion increases. This is consistent with the assumption that parties who are more risk tolerant, utilise 'harder' bargaining tactics and receive greater allocation of benefits or utility (McCarty & Meirowitz, 2007). The axioms that are the foundation of the Nash Bargaining Solution follow the assumption that bargainers are 'playing' to maximise utility; that the bargainers negotiate within the bargaining range (i.e. not in the insult zones) and efficiently allocate available resources; resource allocation is based solely on bargainer's preferences and insult values (or disagreement value); and the solution is not affected by the elimination of resources for other uses (McCarty & Meirowitz, 2007). For a formalised overview of the axioms that are the foundation of the Nash Bargaining Solution see McCarty & Meirowitz, (2008) and for mathematical proof of the solution see Muthoo (1999).

The non-cooperative bargaining theory, as opposed to the Nash bargaining theory, provides a positive theoretical model which deduces the behaviour of actual bargainers (McCarty & Meirowitz, 2007). This model begins with Rubinstein (1982). The Rubinstein bargaining game contemplates a situation where there are two players and an infinite number of offers. Rubenstein uses the example of two players who are deciding how to divide a pie, where the pie has a value of 1. The player's alternate making offers and the game proceeds until an offer is accepted. If no offer is accepted, both players get nothing. Rubinstein's solution showed that while the game has infinite Nash equilibria, there was a distinct subgame perfect equilibrium. The subgame perfect equilibrium implies that if actors have equal discount factors, the player to make the first 'move' has a greater advantage as the second player discounts the future (McCarty & Meirowitz, 2007). Another implication is that when discount rates converge the equilibrium is an equal split of shares. Where players receive an offer that is what they expect, the rejection of an offer would create unsubstantiated delay (McCarty & Meirowitz, 2007). Thus, in these situations where the discount rates converge, an agreement can be made quickly, aligning with the Nash Bargaining Solution (McCarty & Meirowitz, 2007). With an alternating offer set up and a small window of time between offers, the bargainers have almost identical bargaining power, and as such divide the pie in half (McCarty & Meirowitz, 2007). Where, however, only one player is able to make offers, that player has greater bargaining power and can exploit the situation (McCarty & Meirowitz, 2007).

Bargaining theory has been studied extensively in relation to war as a bargaining process (Powell, 2002). To quote Schelling nearly all conflicts "are essentially bargaining situations" (Schelling, 1960 p.5). The international relations theory models the bargaining process of war, again building off of Rubenstein's seminal model (Powell, 2002). Social institutions arise from constraints imposed on others and are dependent upon the power of these influences and ability to constrain others (Knight & Jack, 1992). The value of these institutions is reflected in the ability to attract equilibrium outcomes in strategic conflict (Knight & Jack, 1992). That is, actors can rely on the institutions to structure interactions and develop strategies that result in equilibria that is most desirable to their position across the range of possible outcomes (Knight & Jack, 1992).

\The Zone of Possible Agreement (ZOPA) is a bargaining range of possible outcomes from negotiation (Kim, 2018). It is determined by first establishing insult zones for both the buyer and seller (Kim, 2018). Insult zones refer to the point at which an offer is viewed as insulting (Kim, 2018). The classic example is the negotiation of an employment contract (Kim, 2018). For demonstrative purposes suppose that negotiations are taking place for the employment of a lawyer. The salary is the determinative factor. The lawyer is a senior associate and the average salary for a lawyer, with their level of experience, is $175,000. If the firm's initial offer was $1, this would likely be viewed as insulting to the lawyer. While it may be irrational, and non-economical to form emotional attachment in the process of negotiations, it is human nature. On the other side of negotiations, if the lawyer's first offer, or counteroffer, was $5,000,000 this may be viewed as an insult to the firm. Potentially signalling that the lawyer was not taking the negotiations seriously or signal a lack of industry knowledge, and common sense. These insult zones, at both ends of the range, are the zones at which behaviour is deemed to be so egregious that it would end negotiations (Kim, 2018). Say for example, the lawyer would view anything less than $100,000 as a personal insult, and the firm would deem any offer from the lawyer greater than $300,000 as extreme enough behaviour to halt negotiations. Once these insult zones have been established the next step is to determine the bargaining zone for the buyer and seller (Kim, 2018). The overlap between these bargaining zones is the ZOPA. Within the ZOPA itself there are many bargaining outcomes, this is known as the bargaining zone (Kim, 2018). Strategizing to achieve the best possible outcome within the bargaining zone is the focus of bargaining theory. Calculating this range is useful for contract negotiations and other bargaining situations, such as international negotiations.

Strategic bargaining strategies are informed by expected value (Kim, 2018). Which is a value assigned to the anticipated payout accounting for infinite repetitions (Kim, 2018). To better understand the expected value calculation, consider the classic example of a coin toss. The predicted outcome is 50 percent heads and 50 percent tails based on infinite iterations (Kim, 2018). However, in a situation where person X is told to flip a coin ten times and four out of the ten times the coin landed on heads, the "rational" prediction would be that the next coin toss would land on heads. This is known as the Law of Large Numbers, which provides that with increased iterations the greater convergence between the estimated value and actual outcome (Kim, 2018). The expected value in a gambling scenario can be calculated as the product of the amount of potential gain and the probability of occurrence (Kim, 2018). A study on rational choice theory found that people are more apt to make decisions based not on expected value but rather on the value that would increase convergence between the actual outcomes and the expected value across infinite iterations (Kahneman et al.,1982). This, of course, was not consistent across all participants. Variance between choices was dependent, in part, on risk aversion. Participants that were more risk averse opted for lower returns in exchange for lower risk (Kahneman et al., 1982). In another scenario studied by Kahneman et al. (1982), a gambling situation was framed in terms of potential losses rather than gains. They found that people were more risk averse. This can be explained, primarily by people's desire for financial security. Another gambling scenario in which the participants had to decide between guaranteed loss and the possibility of losing more coupled with the potential to lose less than the alternative, people had a greater tendency to choose the option with greater risk (Kahneman et al., 1982). This finding is consistent with the loss aversion theory which provides that people are willing to take greater risks where there are potential losses. Under rational choice theory, however, there should be no significant difference between these scenarios (Kim, 2018). In practice, there are discernible differences in people's decision-making process and the way scenarios are framed (Kim, 2018). Knowing how to frame persuasive arguments is instrumental to achieving successful outcomes and predicting human behaviour.

These game theories and models can help predict peoples 'moves' in negotiations and inform strategic decision making and allocation of resources. The following chapters will explore the psychological foundations of persuasion and influence at a more individual level and in broader situations, such as international negotiations.

References

Cialdini, R. B. (2001). The science of persuasion. Scientific American, 284(2), 76-81.

Dür, A., & Mateo, G. (2010). Bargaining power and negotiation tactics: The negotiations on the EU's financial perspective, 2007–13. JCMS: Journal of Common Market Studies, 48(3), 557-578.

Gamer, M., Zurowski, B., & Büchel, C. (2010). Different amygdala subregions mediate valence-related and attentional effects of oxytocin in humans. Proceedings of the National Academy of Sciences, 107(20), 9400-9405.

Hardin, G. (1968). The tragedy of the commons: the population problem has no technical solution; it requires a fundamental extension in morality. science, 162(3859), 1243-1248.

Kahneman, D., Slovic, S. P., Slovic, P., & Tversky, A. (Eds.). (1982). Judgment under uncertainty: Heuristics and biases. Cambridge university press.

Kim, J. (2018). Persuasion: The hidden forces that influence negotiations. Routledge.

Knight, J., & Jack, K. (1992). Institutions and social conflict. Cambridge University Press.

McCarty, N., & Meirowitz, A. (2007). Political game theory: an introduction. Cambridge University Press.

Montero-Porras, E., Grujić, J., Fernández Domingos, E., & Lenaerts, T. (2022). Inferring strategies from observations in long iterated Prisoner's dilemma experiments. Scientific reports, 12(1), 1-12.

Muthoo, A. (1999). Bargaining theory with applications. Cambridge University Press.

Northover, S. B., Pedersen, W. C., Cohen, A. B., & Andrews, P. W. (2017). Artificial surveillance cues do not increase generosity: Two meta-analyses. Evolution and Human Behavior, 38(1), 144-153.

Pauwels, L., Declerck, C. H., & Boone, C. (2017). Watching eyes and living up to expectations: Unkind, not kind, eyes increase first mover cooperation in a sequential Prisoner's Dilemma. Games, 8(2), 20.

Poundstone, W. (1993). Prisoner's Dilemma/John Von Neumann, game theory and the puzzle of the bomb. Anchor.

Powell, R. (2002). Bargaining theory and international conflict. Annual Review of Political Science, 5(1), 1-30.

Purzycki, B. G., Apicella, C., Atkinson, Q. D., Cohen, E., McNamara, R. A., Willard, A. K., ... & Henrich, J. (2016). Moralistic gods, supernatural punishment and the expansion of human sociality. Nature, 530(7590), 327-330.

Rubinstein, A. (1982). Perfect equilibrium in a bargaining model. Econometrica: Journal of the Econometric Society, 97-109.

Schelling, T. C. (1960). The Strategy of Conflict Cambridge. Harvard University Press.

Turocy, T., & Stengel, B. (2001). Game Theory-CDAM Research Report LSE-CDAM-2001-09. Centre for Discrete and Applicable Mathematics, London School of Economics & Political Science, London, 12.

Van Dijk, Eric. "The economics of prosocial behavior." The Oxford handbook of prosocial behavior (2015): 86-99.

Chapter: Bargaining Power and International Negotiations

Barry, B. (1980). Is it better to be powerful or lucky?. Political Studies, 28(2), 183-194.

Capacity and Concessions: Bargaining Power in Multilateral Negotiations

Drahos, P. (2003). When the weak bargain with the strong: negotiations in the World Trade Organization. International Negotiation, 8(1), 79-109.

Janusch, H. (2018). The interaction effects of bargaining power: The interplay between veto power, asymmetric interdependence, reputation, and audience costs. Negotiation Journal, 34(3), 219-241.

Kydd, A. H., & McManus, R. W. (2017). Threats and assurances in crisis bargaining. Journal of conflict resolution, 61(2), 325-348.

Panke, D. (2012). Dwarfs in international negotiations: how small states make their voices heard. Cambridge Review of International Affairs, 25(3), 313-328.

Panke, D. (2014). Is Bigger Better? Activity and Success in Negotiations in the United Nations General Assembly. Negotiation Journal, 30(4), 367-392.

Panke, D. (2016). Small states in the European Union: coping with structural disadvantages. Routledge.

Pruitt, D. G. (1983). Strategic choice in negotiation. American Behavioral Scientist, 27(2), 167-194.

Putnam, R. D. (1988). Diplomacy and domestic politics: the logic of two-level games. International organization, 42(3), 427-460.

Rickli, J. M. (2008). European small states' military policies after the Cold War: from territorial to niche strategies. Cambridge review of international affairs, 21(3), 307-325.

Schneider, C. J. (2011). Weak states and institutionalized bargaining power in international organizations. International Studies Quarterly, 55(2), 331-355.

Schneider, G. (2005). Capacity and concessions: Bargaining power in multilateral negotiations. Millennium, 33(3), 665-689.

Steinberg, R. H. (2002). In the shadow of law or power? Consensus-based bargaining and outcomes in the GATT/WTO. International organization, 56(2), 339-374.

Chapter: The Psychological Foundations of Persuasion and Influence

Albarracin, D., & Shavitt, S. (2018). Attitudes and attitude change. Annual review of psychology, 69(1), 299-327.

Aronson, E., Willerman, B., & Floyd, J. (1966). The effect of a pratfall on increasing interpersonal attractiveness. Psychonomic Science, 4(6), 227-228.

Barnes Jr, J. H. (1984). Cognitive biases and their impact on strategic planning. Strategic Management Journal, 5(2), 129-137.

Buckley, K. E., & Anderson, C. A. (2012). A theoretical model of the effects and consequences of playing video games. In P. Vorderer & J. Bryant (Eds.), Playing video games: Motives, responses, and consequences (pp. 363–378). Lawrence Erlbaum Associates Publishers.

Calbi, M., Langiulli, N., Siri, F., Umiltà, M. A., & Gallese, V. (2021). Visual exploration of emotional body language: a behavioural and eye-tracking study. Psychological Research, 85(6), 2326-2339.

Druckman, J. N. (2022). A Framework for the Study of Persuasion. Annual Review of Political Science, 25, 65-88.

Feinberg, M., & Willer, R. (2013). The moral roots of environmental attitudes. Psychological science, 24(1), 56-62.

Fishbach, A., & Touré-Tillery, M. (2013). Goals and motivation. Noba Textbook Series: Psychology.

Fiske, S. T., & Taylor, S. E. (2013). Social cognition: From brains to culture. Sage.

Goldstein, M. (2022). U.S. government to jury in 1MDB trial: Convict even if you don't believe our star witness. New York Times.

Greitemeyer, T. (2009). Effects of songs with prosocial lyrics on prosocial behavior: Further evidence and a mediating mechanism. Personality and Social Psychology Bulletin, 35(11), 1500-1511.

Hamden, N. & Tan, R. (2019). Jho Low a master manipulator, says Najib's ex-aide. The Star.

Hart, W., Albarracín, D., Eagly, A. H., Brechan, I., Lindberg, M. J., & Merrill, L. (2009). Feeling validated versus being correct: a meta-analysis of selective exposure to information. Psychological bulletin, 135(4), 555.

Holtfreter, K., Van Slyke, S., Bratton, J., & Gertz, M. (2008). Public perceptions of white-collar crime and punishment. Journal of Criminal Justice, 36(1), 50-60.

Jacob, C., Guéguen, N., Ardiccioni, R., & Sénémeaud, C. (2013). Exposure to altruism quotes and tipping behavior in a restaurant. International Journal of Hospitality Management, 32, 299-301.

Levi, M. (2006). The media construction of financial white-collar crimes. British journal of criminology, 46(6), 1037-1057.

Lynn, M. (2015). Service gratuities and tipping: A motivational framework. Journal of Economic Psychology, 46, 74-88.

Macpherson, W. (1920). The psychology of persuasion. Routledge.

Mahtani, S. (2018). Former Malaysian prime minister Najib Razak charged in corruption probe: Najib was under investigation for billions misappropriated from the 1MDB investment fund. The Washington Post.

Mallet V. & Palma S. (2019). Najib Razak defiant over 1MDB corruption claims. Financial Times.

Markovich, Z., Baum, M. A., Berinsky, A. J., de Benedictis-Kessner, J., & Yamamoto, T. (2020). Dynamic persuasion: decay and accumulation of partisan media persuasion. In Annual Meeting of the Southern Political Science Association, Jan (Vol. 9, No. 11).

McGinley, H., McGinley, P., & Nicholas, K. (1978). Smiling, body position, and interpersonal attraction. Bulletin of the psychonomic Society, 12(1), 21-24.

Ngui, Y., & Hope, B. (2016). Malaysia Won't Interfere With Foreign 1MDB Legal Action; Government won't protect citizens, senior government official says. Wall Street Journal.

Petty, R. E., & Cacioppo, J. T. (1986). The elaboration likelihood model of persuasion. In Communication and persuasion (pp. 1-24). Springer, New York, NY.

Pratto, F., & John, O. P. (1991). Automatic vigilance: the attention-grabbing power of negative social information. Journal of personality and social psychology, 61(3), 380.

Rahimi Y. (2019). Jho Low was Najib's 'unofficial' advisor, says witness. The Malaysian Reserve.

Reuters Staff (2020). China denies harboring 1MDB fugitive Jho Low. Reuters.

Righi, S., Gronchi, G., Marzi, T., Rebai, M., & Viggiano, M. P. (2015). You are that smiling guy I met at the party! Socially positive signals foster memory for identities and contexts. Acta psychologica, 159, 1-7.

Stanley, M. L., Whitehead, P. S., & Marsh, E. J. (2022). The cognitive processes underlying false beliefs. Journal of Consumer Psychology, 32(2), 359-369.

Tamir, D. I., & Mitchell, J. P. (2012). Disclosing information about the self is intrinsically rewarding. Proceedings of the National Academy of Sciences, 109(21), 8038-8043.

Tesler, M., & Zaller, J. (2017). The power of political communication. The Oxford handbook of political communication, 69.

The Edge Markets (2017). Jho Low gave at least US$200m to celebs' charities.

Wardekker, J. A., Petersen, A. C., & van Der Sluijs, J. P. (2009). Ethics and public perception of climate change: Exploring the Christian voices in the US public debate. Global Environmental Change, 19(4), 512-521.

Wright, T., Hope, B. (2018). Billion dollar whale : the man who fooled Wall Street, Hollywood, and the world. Hachette Books.

Chapter 5: The Psychological Foundations of Persuasion and Influence

The study of persuasion is rudimentary to understanding society and the new language of leadership and business in a market-driven global economy. This chapter on the psychology of persuasion will look at the process of persuasion, best-practice strategies, mechanisms that impact one's perception of others and a look into white collar crime and the influence of media on the perception of different crimes.

Humans are not rational actors, emotion and instinct play a significant role in decision-making. In fact, persuasion is dominated by irrational elements, founded on desire and preconceived beliefs about the way things should be (Macpherson, 1920). The success of persuasion is proportionate to the strength of this belief. This belief is further strengthened when others are persuaded (Macpherson, 1920). Persuasion can be separated into self persuasion and persuasion of others. This chapter will focus primarily on the persuasion of others, that is the deliberate and quasi systematic process in which one tries to imprint beliefs on others (Macpherson, 1920). Self-persuasion, in contrast, is the unconscious process which is rooted in remote factors (Macpherson, 1920).

The way situations are presented, in the process of persuasion, can be described as narration (Macpherson, 1920). Techniques that play into listeners emotion, sentiments and instincts can be utilised to one's advantage. It is crucial that the narration is coherent, complete, and tailored to the desired audience in a way that appeals to their emotion. The study of persuasion dates back to Aristotle (Barnes, 1984). However, the literature lacks cohesiveness and is often contradictory and/or disconnected. Attempts to resolve inconsistencies in research has focused on establishing frameworks for more cohesive research. This chapter will highlight some of the inconsistencies in the research on persuasion but will focus largely on generalised techniques to better advance arguments and prime receivers to achieve successful persuasion outcomes. The Elaboration Likelihood Model is a prominent psychological process theory that provides a framework for the categorization and study of processes that are the basis of effective persuasion (Petty & Cacioppo, 1986). The model outlines two pathways to persuasion (Petty & Cacioppo, 1986). The first being the central route, which requires active thought processes and the second being the peripheral route which is linked to inferences people make in response to cues in the persuasion environment (Petty & Cacioppo, 1986). These two pathways result in different outcomes. The central route being the dominant predictor of consistent responses (Petty & Cacioppo, 1986). This model provides valuable insight into the process of persuasion but lacks critical considerations in the persuasion process such as competition and the speaker's motivation to persuade (Druckman, 2022).

Druckman (2022) provides a good framework for research on generalised persuasion based on four dimensions: actors, treatments, outcomes, and settings. For the purposes of this section the process of persuasion and its study can be broken down, by its actors: speakers and receivers. The study persuasion from the receiver can be characterised as the target and how persuasive attempts influence the target's attitudes (Druckman, 2022). This is best evaluated as the weighted sum of the receiver's beliefs about the object or idea. This incorporates both positive and negative beliefs and are measured by their relative magnitude and weight (Druckman, 2022). The success of a persuasion is dependent on these pre-existing attitudes, motivation for the end result and the energy exerted into coming to that particular decision. The energy exerted, or effort, that an individual invests into assessing the communicated message. Effort exerted is dependent on the availability of information and the salience of topics. Where the perceived speaker credibility is greater, receivers will exert less effort in scrutinising the communicated message (Druckman, 2022). Receivers are motivated by goals, even where the process requires minimal conscious deliberation (Toure-Tillery & Fishbach, 2013). People engage in behaviour that is consistent with previously held beliefs and respond to cues in their immediate environment that influence the behaviour they engage in. Cues related to people's goals or values can prime decision making (Toure-Tillery & Fishbach, 2013).

This section will highlight some specific techniques that people, and corporations can utilise to help persuade others. This includes the elicitation of self speech, disclosing weaknesses, body language, timing, and consideration of individual preferences and people's aversion to risk. These techniques will prime the discussion of framing strategies and ways to optimise the success of persuasion outcomes in different environments. Framing narration in a way that aligns with the receiver's belief system can assist in the success of persuasion. People desire consistency in their beliefs, as posited by Stanley et al. (2002), this motivation for consistency is driven by the desire to maintain social identity. Similarly, people are influenced by value affirmation (Druckman, 2022). This has been researched primarily in relation to policy making, scientific communication and politics. A study by Feinberg and Willer (2013), acknowledged the polarisation of attitudes towards environmental issues and looked at ways to reframe environmental issues in way that reduced the attitude polarisation between liberals and conservatives. They found that when environmental issues were framed in a way that appealed to the themes of purity and sanctity it encouraged better communication between parties and reduced the attitude gap (Feinberg & Willer, 2013).

Another study found that when environmental issues were framed in a way that appealed to morality and religion they were more successful at persuading individuals that identify as conservative (Wardekker et al., 2009). Understanding the political and religious environment can help inform persuasion strategies. Further, allowing the person you are trying to persuade to speak about themselves may increase persuasion effectiveness. Human speech output is 30-40% communicating subjective experiences (Tamir & Mitchell, 2012). A study by Tamir and Mitchell (2012) showed that speaking about oneself increases internal reward processes in a way similar to sex, money and food incentives. Introspection was enough to signal greater activity in brain regions associated with reward. fMRI machines showed that the regions of the brain associated with motivation and reward increased activity when the participant spoke about themselves publicly (Tamir & Mitchell, 2012). Factors such as intimacy of disclosure and reciprocation impacted the likelihood of self disclosure. By allowing others the opportunity to self disclose information, feelings or thoughts to others, one can benefit from the performance advantages that result. Eliciting feedback, for example, can be used to engender better relationships, trust, and achieve desired outcomes in the persuasion process. Appealing to the "pratfall effect", the phenomena that disclosing one's weaknesses increases both their likability and trustworthiness, can be an effective persuasion strategy (Aronson et al.,1996). However, a crucial caveat to this is that the person must first be believed to be a competent person (Aronson et al.,1996). The rationale behind the pratfall effect is that a person with greater intellectual ability, relative to the observer, is viewed as distant, as such, exposing one's weakness humanises that person and therefore increases their attractiveness (Aronson et al.,1996). In contrast, when someone the observer views as equal or lesser, in intellectual ability, discloses a weakness this is detrimental to their character (Aronson et al.,1996). In practice then, it is crucial to identify and study the audience to determine whether the disclosure of a weakness may benefit the narration. This includes estimation of the audience's preconceived beliefs about the competency of the speaker.

The stereotype content model is a theoretical framework that maps social perception based on warmth and competence. These character traits heavily influence emotion, and thus, persuasion strategy. Warmth is associated with trustworthiness, friendliness, and sincerity (Fiske & Taylor, 2013). Whereas competence is linked to intellectual ability, skill, and efficiency (Fiske & Taylor, 2013). If the speaker has a high relative competency score compared to warmth, disclosing one's weaknesses can increase the trustworthiness of the speaker by appealing to the pratfall effect. Body language has been studied extensively in relation to interpersonal attraction. Strategies informed by evidence of effective body language communication are valuable to persuasion and negotiation strategies. McGinley et al. (1978) shows that the women who smile more are viewed as more attractive. Attractiveness was also found to increase when displaying open, rather than closed, body positions. Smiling was the most influential body language for interpersonal attraction (McGinley et al.,1978). An experiment that tracked eye movement determined that the subjects spent more time focused on the upper region of the speaker's body (Calbri et al., 2020). This may be, in part, why interpersonal attraction is influenced, significantly, by smiling. Interestingly, the greater the facial strain to smile the more people perceived others as likeable and trustworthy (Righi et al., 2015). Thus, a persuasion strategy should integrate body language that communicates the desired outcome or primes the receiver for later communications.

When framing narration speakers should be cognizant of timing (Druckman, 2002). Well framed opening statements are critical to set the pace for further arguments. People place a high value on the consistency of their beliefs and deploy defensive cognitive processes when evidence refutes these beliefs (Hart et al., 2009). It is thus crucial that the initial argument is framed in a way that is consistent with previously held beliefs. Where the initial information aligns with existing values, people exert less reasoning effort when provided with more information (Hart et al., 2009). Even where this 'new' information may contradict their values or beliefs (Albarracin & Shavitt, 2018). People place particular emphasis in certain situations that are a perceived threat to their social identity (Druckman, 2022). For example, topics on gun control, abortion, and COVID-19 are particularly partisan and elicit directional processes. Kim (2018) raises concerns about the impact of social media and tailored news on individual decision-making processes. The impact of media and issue framing will be further explored in relation to white collar crime.

While priming the receiver with cues and/or information may assist with successful outcomes, the persuasive message is more convincing where there is an element of immediacy (Druckman, 2022). In a study on voting behaviour, it was found that the effects of persuasion are limited in duration (Tesler & Zaller, 2017). Other studies, however, have found that the effects of persuasion persist (Markovich et al., 2020). Markovich et al. (2020) found that the effects on the attitudes towards partisan media endured even after a single exposure. Further, they found that the additive effect from repeated exposure to persuasive narration had little impact on attitudes. Perhaps what differentiates the results in these studies is the content of the persuasive message. The study by Markovich et al. (2002) researched the effect of partisan media, thus it may be that where the persuasive narration is on topics that are typically very polarised, initial arguments can drive polarisation. Whereas with other content, the initial argument may only have a short-term effect and need to be reinforced to create a cumulative effect on attitudes towards the topic. The pernicious effects of consumer self selection of information can inform political and public policy strategies. Prospect theory, for example, shows that people are more apt to make decisions to avoid a negative rather than positive experience. Research shows that less cognitive resources are allocated in response to positive personality traits than negative ones (Pratto & John, 1991). This is consistent with other research on the asymmetry of individuals's evaluations of loss aversion and potential gains. Evolutionary reasons support this asymmetry in reactions (Pratto & John, 1991). Risk aversion is associated with a sense of urgency and negative effects signal that an adjustment to current state is necessary (Pratto & John, 1991).

Further, group pressure can help persuade individuals. People organise into groups, professionally, religiously and politically because of shared values and beliefs. It is efficient to short-cut individual thought processes and engage in collective thinking. Even where an individual may otherwise resist the majority opinion there is often pressure to conform to the common belief/ opinion (Kim, 2018). Continued behaviour that runs contrary to membership may create distance and/or result in removal from the group (Kim, 2018). The fear of this consequence and alienation from the group promotes group conformity and more uniform behaviour/rationalisation (Kim, 2018). While there are certainly disadvantages to a society that thinks and behaves collectively, it can be used to one's advantage in the process of persuasion and strategizing. People, as members of a group, have more collective power. The majority of individuals have very little power to exert influence over others. However, most people desire power, and are willing to sacrifice some degree of individual thought/behaviour for greater collective power (Kim, 2018). Thus, in the process of persuasion, organising as a group to create more collective power and therefore exert more influence on others, can help maximise potential for successful bargaining outcomes.

The study of human psychology and the mental shortcuts people make in their judgements can help inform the psychological foundations of persuasion and guide strategies to optimise influence strategies. Priming is an unconscious association that can influence rational behaviour (Kim, 2018). Even where the priming effects are not apparent, for example music playing in the background or images displayed on the wall, cues can influence behaviour (Kim, 2018). For example, a study on consumer behaviour and service gratuities found that priming customers with altruism and love increased the amount that people tipped (Lynn, 2015). The rationale is called spreading of activation which describes the assumption that a belief connects to a network of other associated information (Jacob et al., 2013). Altruistic quotes on bills were shown to increase customer generosity when tipping (Jacob et al., 2013). This supports the concept of spreading activation. That is, when an individual is exposed to altruistic cues other concepts including generosity are activated resulting in increased monetary tips (Jacob et al., 2013).

Prosocial lyrics, as another example, have been shown to increase prosocial behaviour (Greitemeyer, 2009). The General Learning Model describes an episodic learning structure (Buckley & Anderson, 2012). Repetition of information, under this model, becomes more accessible and eventually automatized (Buckley & Anderson, 2012). The reinforcement of information affects one's personality and provokes the trigger of certain behaviours in response to various stimuli (Buckley & Anderson, 2012). While the study by Greitemeyer (2009) did not examine the long-term effect of repeated exposure to altruistic songs, it provides empirical evidence of the interconnectedness between altruism, empathy, and generous behaviour. For the purposes of persuasion, both long-term and short-term strategies can promote successful outcomes. Repeated exposure to cues that will trigger the desired outcome is ideal, but where this is not possible, cues that are already associated with desired behaviour may influence the outcome. For example, if the goal is to persuade individuals to donate to a charitable organisation, visual or audio cues that are associated with empathy or altruistic behaviour may increase the generosity of patrons.

Persuasion can, and often is, used for morally repugnant behaviours. This section will explore crimes of persuasion, the factors that contribute to the presence of fraud in society, and a brief discussion on the disparity between how society views white collar crimes from other crimes committed. The strategies for successful persuasion and the public perception of white-collar crime can be applied to a case study of Jho Low.

Jho Low, a Malaysian financier behind the multibillion-dollar investment scandal appealed to people's desire for extravagant living, successfully persuading the rich and famous of his success as a businessman (Goldstein, 2022). The scandal indicted Goldman Sachs bankers and Najib Razak (former Prime Minister of Malaysia) (Mahtani, 2018). Jho Low was able to persuade the world of his wealth and intelligence and embezzle billions of dollars in collusion with some of the world's largest banks, auditors and investors (Ngui & Hope, 2016). Under the guise of Malaysia's national investment fund 1Malaysia Development Berhad (1MDB) Jho Low, previously only the title of "special advisor" at 1MDB, he was able to persuade others to raise billions of dollars, and embezzle over $4.5 billion through American banks (Rahimi, 2019). $731 million went to Razak's personal accounts (Mallet & Palma, 2019). Jho Low, himself was accused of personally profiting close to $1 billion from the funds (Goldstein, 2022) Amhari Efendi Nazaruddin, former aid to the prime minister Razak, described Jho Low as a "master manipulator" who was able to manipulate people with his charisma and persuasive techniques (Hamdan & Tan, 2019). The case raised questions about need for independent auditors and brought the legitimacy of Deloitte, KPMG, and PwC auditors into question (Ngui & Hope, 2016). While Malaysian news sources may not display an accurate picture of Razak's and Nazaruddin's role in the 1MDB scandal, it is apparent that Jho Low with the help of other corrupt officials was the key player in the scandal. Low has been able to successfully evade detention and maintains a life of luxury as a fugitive in China (Reuters Staff, 2020). Ironically the embezzled money was used to finance The Wolf of Wall Street, a movie about white collar crime, a Martin Scorsese film (Goldstein, 2022).

White collar crime bears significant economic costs, creates distrust in corporations and can cause significant harm to its victims. However, the story of Jho Low is portrayed in the media like a money heist story. The book Billion Dollar Whale describes Low as a young, driven man who shocked the financial industry (Wright & Hope, 2018). Jho Low has even been described as a modern-day Robin Hood, donating over $200 million USD to charities such as Panthera, Keep A Child Alive, the University of Texas MD Anderson Cancer Center the United Nations Foundation, the National Geographic Pristine Seas fund, and the Children's National Hospital (The Edge Markets, 2017). These donations were all donated to celebrities that Low paid to party with (Goldstein, 2022). The public perceives white collar crime differently than violent crimes (Holtfreter et al., 2008). This is largely because of peoples perceived threat and severity of victimisation (Holtfreter et al., 2008). Evidently, this is largely influenced by media coverage.

Levi (2006) attributes this to the tendency of mass media to cover financial fraud in a way similar to that of entertainment news. He observed that the reporting of white-collar crime generally focuses on the individual and their motivation, and issues in the past or present that may help explain why they committed fraud in a sympathetic manner. Typically, these news stories criticise the systems that enabled the fraud to take place rather than the individual that took advantage of the systems. The study of the representation of white-collar crime in the media is important to understand how financial fraud continues to be so prevalent. It is also important to consider the differences between the prestige and social status of offenders. Most economic crimes in the US were "blue-collar" crimes. However, the crimes that receive the most media and public attention are white-collar crimes. In part, because they often involve multiple high-status people and/or corporations. Offenders with high social status are also in a better position to pay for good defences and media campaigns. With the availability of a wealth of information online, consumers are interested in 'personalities' (Levi, 2006).

Where the offender has a personality, like Jho Low, who otherwise has likeable traits, people are more apt to blame the 'Establishment' rather than the individual. People look up to those that have achieved the status, prestige, or luxuries that they desire. Jho Low is an example of someone who lived an extravagant lifestyle, partying with celebrities, and other elites, a lifestyle that people admire. Jho Low has a short stature, is large, chubby cheeked and charismatic. Going back to the pratfall effect as discussed by Aronson et al. (1996), where a speaker is viewed as highly competent, they can benefit from exposing their weaknesses. Jho Low's appearance might have been part of the reason he was so likeable by many. His appearance, which would arguably be detrimental to someone who lacked competence, portrayed innocence, and engendered the trust of others who may otherwise viewed him as distant. While it is a small subset of white-collar crimes that receive the same media attention as the 1MDB scandal, these are the cases that receive wider public attention. The media attention alone, often already resembles entertainment news, and this is furthered when films and books are produced based on the case. Movies such as the film on Enron, 'Catch Me If You Can', and the 'Rogue Trader', further the idolization of white-collar criminals by developing their character (Levi, 2006). These films lack technical details of the case and instead focus on the individual 'characters' involved in the scandal and the loopholes that enabled them to take advantage of the system.

Understanding how people are influenced and persuaded by others, corporations and the media is an important consideration for developing strategies to discourage financial fraud and reduce economic impact. The strategies for persuasion discussed earlier in this chapter can be utilised on an individual level to maximise profit, social prestige, and engender better relationships. They can also be advanced to inform public policy decisions, encourage conformity, and influence the outcome in international negotiations, as discussed later in the book. There are obvious moral and ethical dilemmas with persuasion strategies that are used to enable individuals to take advantage of other's weaknesses and/or the weaknesses of corporations and/or establishments. Jho Low was able to gain the trust of others under the guise of legitimate business dealings. He is an example of how persuasion strategies can be used for morally repugnant behaviour. The case study also points to a greater issue of media coverage, financial fraud and the significant financial burden that white-collar crime bears on its victims and on society as a whole.

References

Albarracin, D., & Shavitt, S. (2018). Attitudes and attitude change. Annual review of psychology, 69(1), 299-327.

Aronson, E., Willerman, B., & Floyd, J. (1966). The effect of a pratfall on increasing interpersonal attractiveness. Psychonomic Science, 4(6), 227-228.

Barnes Jr, J. H. (1984). Cognitive biases and their impact on strategic planning. Strategic Management Journal, 5(2), 129-137.

Buckley, K. E., & Anderson, C. A. (2012). A theoretical model of the effects and consequences of playing video games. In P. Vorderer & J. Bryant (Eds.), Playing video games: Motives, responses, and consequences (pp. 363–378). Lawrence Erlbaum Associates Publishers.

Calbi, M., Langiulli, N., Siri, F., Umiltà, M. A., & Gallese, V. (2021). Visual exploration of emotional body language: a behavioural and eye-tracking study. Psychological Research, 85(6), 2326-2339.

Druckman, J. N. (2022). A Framework for the Study of Persuasion. Annual Review of Political Science, 25, 65-88.

Feinberg, M., & Willer, R. (2013). The moral roots of environmental attitudes. Psychological science, 24(1), 56-62.

Fishbach, A., & Touré-Tillery, M. (2013). Goals and motivation. Noba Textbook Series: Psychology.

Fiske, S. T., & Taylor, S. E. (2013). Social cognition: From brains to culture. Sage.

Goldstein, M. (2022). U.S. government to jury in 1MDB trial: Convict even if you don't believe our star witness. New York Times.

Greitemeyer, T. (2009). Effects of songs with prosocial lyrics on prosocial behavior: Further evidence and a mediating mechanism. Personality and Social Psychology Bulletin, 35(11), 1500-1511.

Hamden, N. & Tan, R. (2019). Jho Low a master manipulator, says Najib's ex-aide. The Star.

Hart, W., Albarracín, D., Eagly, A. H., Brechan, I., Lindberg, M. J., & Merrill, L. (2009). Feeling validated versus being correct: a meta-analysis of selective exposure to information. Psychological bulletin, 135(4), 555.

Holtfreter, K., Van Slyke, S., Bratton, J., & Gertz, M. (2008). Public perceptions of white-collar crime and punishment. Journal of Criminal Justice, 36(1), 50-60.

Jacob, C., Guéguen, N., Ardiccioni, R., & Sénémeaud, C. (2013). Exposure to altruism quotes and tipping behavior in a restaurant. International Journal of Hospitality Management, 32, 299-301.

Levi, M. (2006). The media construction of financial white-collar crimes. British journal of criminology, 46(6), 1037-1057.

Lynn, M. (2015). Service gratuities and tipping: A motivational framework. Journal of Economic Psychology, 46, 74-88.

Macpherson, W. (1920). The psychology of persuasion. Routledge.

Mahtani, S. (2018). Former Malaysian prime minister Najib Razak charged in corruption probe: Najib was under investigation for billions misappropriated from the 1MDB investment fund. The Washington Post.

Mallet V. & Palma S. (2019). Najib Razak defiant over 1MDB corruption claims. Financial Times.

Markovich, Z., Baum, M. A., Berinsky, A. J., de Benedictis-Kessner, J., & Yamamoto, T. (2020). Dynamic persuasion: decay and accumulation of partisan media persuasion. In Annual Meeting of the Southern Political Science Association, Jan (Vol. 9, No. 11).

McGinley, H., McGinley, P., & Nicholas, K. (1978). Smiling, body position, and interpersonal attraction. Bulletin of the psychonomic Society, 12(1), 21-24.

Ngui, Y., & Hope, B. (2016). Malaysia Won't Interfere With Foreign 1MDB Legal Action; Government won't protect citizens, senior government official says. Wall Street Journal.

Petty, R. E., & Cacioppo, J. T. (1986). The elaboration likelihood model of persuasion. In Communication and persuasion (pp. 1-24). Springer, New York, NY.

Pratto, F., & John, O. P. (1991). Automatic vigilance: the attention-grabbing power of negative social information. Journal of personality and social psychology, 61(3), 380.

Rahimi Y. (2019). Jho Low was Najib's 'unofficial' advisor, says witness. The Malaysian Reserve.

Reuters Staff (2020). China denies harboring 1MDB fugitive Jho Low. Reuters.

Righi, S., Gronchi, G., Marzi, T., Rebai, M., & Viggiano, M. P. (2015). You are that smiling guy I met at the party! Socially positive signals foster memory for identities and contexts. Acta psychologica, 159, 1-7.

Stanley, M. L., Whitehead, P. S., & Marsh, E. J. (2022). The cognitive processes underlying false beliefs. Journal of Consumer Psychology, 32(2), 359-369.

Tamir, D. I., & Mitchell, J. P. (2012). Disclosing information about the self is intrinsically rewarding. Proceedings of the National Academy of Sciences, 109(21), 8038-8043.

Tesler, M., & Zaller, J. (2017). The power of political communication. The Oxford handbook of political communication, 69.

The Edge Markets (2017). Jho Low gave at least US$200m to celebs' charities.

Wardekker, J. A., Petersen, A. C., & van Der Sluijs, J. P. (2009). Ethics and public perception of climate change: Exploring the Christian voices in the US public debate. Global Environmental Change, 19(4), 512-521.

Wright, T., Hope, B. (2018). Billion dollar whale : the man who fooled Wall Street, Hollywood, and the world. Hachette Books.

Chapter 6: Bargaining Power and International Negotiations

International negotiations rely on bargaining strategies. With increasing international organisations and systems, the study of bargaining strategies and power in relation to international negotiations has become an active area of research. This chapter will focus on bargaining power as a key determinant of international negotiation outcomes and discuss strategies such as the manipulation of threat-potential using lock-in strategies, reliance on non-governmental secretariats and chairs, and role specialisation. These topics will be approached by looking at theoretical and analytical frameworks, with a brief discussion on the applicability of the Nash Bargaining Theory in international negotiations. These strategies can help smaller state actors to better engage in the international regime and predict bargaining outcomes.

The success of international negotiations is dependent upon relative bargaining power. Power can loosely be defined as the amount of influence exerted in a negotiation (Schneider, 2005). Some theorists have pointed out the contribution of luck to bargaining outcomes (Barry, 1980). The study of bargaining and power manipulation can reduce reliance on luck. Bargaining power is not synonymous with material power, contrary to the realist belief that bargaining power in international negotiations is a linear, positive relationship with political and economic power (Schnieder, 2005). Models that exclusively measure bargaining power, on the basis of capability, often calculated by relative economic size, are not consistent with data and fail to explain many bargaining outcomes in international negotiations (Schneider, 2005). The relative material power of the negotiating parties is the first step to establishing an appropriate bargaining strategy. However, other considerations such as state credibility, international and domestic norms and specialisations are critical considerations for bargaining strategies and predicting outcomes (Schneider, 2005).

Despite significant obstacles smaller states encounter in international negotiations, they are still able to engage effectively in international negotiation and have successful bargaining outcomes (Panke, 2012). Weaker states are more easily coerced into contracting for outcomes that, while still Pareto- improving, distribution is weighed in favour of the more powerful actor (Steinberg, 2002). More powerful actors are able to coerce weaker parties into consensus via exit tactics (Steinberg, 2002). If international organisations lose powerful actors, they lose legitimacy and often a new organisation will be formed that better benefits the exiting actors (Steinberg, 2002). Characterising bargaining strategies that advance a state actor's bargaining power can help weaker parties, who may not otherwise have viable alternatives, be successful negotiators. These strategies can help better forecast bargaining outcomes and allow smaller countries to have a seat in the international regime.

The starting point for developing bargaining strategies for international negotiations should involve a complete assessment of state capabilities, often referred to as their "size" in negotiations (Panke, 2012). A small state is defined by some deficit in power owing to their reduced capacity to mobilise resources (Rickli, 2008). Measuring state size is context dependent and will often involve some measure of economic, military, or political power and geographic size or measure of voter distribution (Panke, 2012). These are situational, and the measure of state size should be based on the negotiating circumstances to best determine what measure serves as the best proxy for determining relative power. In this sense, the bargaining power that state actors possess is represented by the power exercised and dependent on the measure used (Rickli, 2008). A state actor can be powerful in one area, such as economic power, while being geographically small (Panke, 2012).

Where distributive effects are at play, determination of state capability is often measured by their economic power. Market size, for example, can provide a good approximation for bargaining power in trade negotiations (Steinberg, 2002). Where there is the potential for armed conflict or in the realm of security policy, state size is measured by relative military and political power (Rickli,

2008). Security policies for small state actors are informed by the need to protect autonomy and maximise influence (Rickli, 2008). Where it is unclear what the best measure for state size is in the negotiating circumstance, measuring the financial resources of state actors can provide a good estimation of state size (Panke, 2012). Effective participation in international negotiations rely on the state's financial resources (Panke, 2012). Budget size determines the number of governmental and negotiation development positions, size of delegations and availability of external advice (Panke, 2012). States that lack budgetary means to effectively engage in international negotiation, will face significant barriers developing negotiation strategies, accessing information and expertise, and ultimately achieving successful bargaining outcomes (Panke, 2012). Smaller state actors must therefore engage in strategies that allow them to manipulate their threat potential via reliance on international law and/or international and domestic norms (Panke, 2012). Other actors can provide support to smaller countries and allow them to better prepare and position themselves at the bargaining table. A country's GDP can serve as a good estimation of available financial resources (Panke, 2012). The value of goods and services is proportional to tax revenue and therefore a good estimation of state budget available for ministerial staff, delegations, external advice, and other support (Panke, 2012). In trade bargaining, threats of market closure or agreements to open markets are often part of negotiation and are essentially the trade currency (Steinberg, 2002). Proportionately, trade liberalisation offers greater domestic benefit to smaller countries via greater relative welfare and employment (Steinberg, 2002). However, the threat of market closure is generally more significant to less developed economies absent specialised resources (Steinberg, 2002). Understanding how to measure relative state capacity can inform bargaining strategies, identify smaller actors in international negotiations, and predict bargaining outcomes. Measuring relative bargaining power of state actors is thus measured by the capacity to influence the behaviour of other states while simultaneously resisting others from altering their behaviour (Rickli, 2008).

Identifying areas of particular importance is especially important for smaller states and allows for resource prioritisation and allocation (Panke, 2012). Once areas of significance are identified small states can better position themselves for strategy development and implementation (Panke, 2012). The relative bargaining power of negotiating parties is largely a social construction dependent on perceived plausibility of threat actualization (Panke, 2014). The strength of bargaining power is proportionate to the threat's credibility. Lock-in strategies can advance the credibility of state actors and minimise the strength of seemingly powerful actors in negotiation (Panke, 2014). One strategy is to link the issue to international law, domestic norms, or existing domestic commitments. This is referred to as a lock-in strategy (Panke, 2014). This strategy is premised on the receiving party's fear of damaging their reputation domestically and/or internationally (Panke, 2014). Reputation is hampered when continued resistance violates international law or is inconsistent with domestic norms (Panke, 2014). This institutionalisation results in a "mature anarchy" system where the international and domestic norms result in a greater than zero-sum game (Rickli, 2008).

Smaller state actors can offset deficits in power by utilising defensive or cooperative bargaining strategies (Rickli, 2008). This law-based approach can better allow smaller states to balance state autonomy and their ability to influence the behaviour of other states (Rickli, 2008). This strategy leverages the initiating actor's threat credibility by reinforcing their position with existing commitments. When effectively done, the receiving actor is entrapped and unable to pursue their prior negotiating position (Panke, 2012). This occasionally leads to the receiving party supporting the issue at hand (Panke, 2012). The effectiveness of this strategy depends, in part, on the number of other states that align with the position. Members of international regimes and/or organisations can better offset size disadvantages, especially if they are long time members (Panke, 2012). Another strategy smaller states can use to advance their position in negotiation is by gaining insight into the position of the opposing state and background information on the issue at hand. Institutional actors can cut costs while allowing states to develop and frame bargaining strategies (Panke, 2012). Non-governmental organisations, and other actors such as industry lobbyists can provide scientific insight, policy advice and background information cost effectively (Panke, 2012). However, these resources are not equally available to all states, and are more difficult for corrupt regimes to take advantage of (Panke, 2012). Internationally, reputation damages are more significant if the state in question can be singled out as an outlier (Panke, 2012). Smaller states can take advantage of this and manipulate threat potential via international law and domestic/international norms (Panke, 2012).

Framing the argument in a matter that resonates with the receiving party can help receptivity (Panke, 2012). For example, framing the argument in a way that appeals to morals instead of a technical argument. In fact, it is easier for smaller states to re-frame their arguments, manipulating the negotiation process, as they are perceived as having fewer individual interests at stake and able to more persuasively argue that they are acting with a common interest (Drahos, 2003). Individuals can then advance their own interests under the guise of a broader issue (Panke, 2012). Smaller states have more pressure to prioritise the allocation of their resources. Role specialisation strategies can also be used to advance smaller states. Becoming experts in a distinct policy area can advance their positions with causal arguments. Research suggests that actors with a reputation of high scientific knowledge are more persuasive (Panke, 2012). Scientific and technical arguments can help frame arguments as a policy decision (Panke, 2012). Smaller states often have information deficits and prioritisation is necessary for successful outcomes in causal, technical arguments (Panke, 2012). In military regimes, cooperative strategies better protect smaller actors' contribution (Putnam, 1988). Contribution depends upon the strategic goals of the operation and the strategic goal of a small state is measured by the degree of influence on other states in an alliance or coalition (Putnam, 1988).

The dominant bargaining strategy is dependent on the range of possible outcomes. If the bargaining problem is a zero-sum game, that is a win-lose game, then parties have no incentive to cooperate, and bargaining strategies tend to be more aggressive (Dur & Mateo, 2010). Most international negotiations, however, have the potential for a mutually beneficial outcome, and are greater than zero-sum games. Further, some outcomes will have a negative payoff for one or both of the parties. This section will focus on the distribution of gains in bargaining outcomes, reasons for asymmetries in outcomes and strategies for optimal outcomes within bargaining ranges. Where the nature of the bargaining problem creates a zero-sum game, the parties should generally utilise a distributive (division of resources) bargaining strategy rather than an integrative (creates value) strategy (Dur & Mateo, 2010). In contrast, where both parties could potentially benefit from the bargaining outcome, the dominant strategy is typically integrative (Dur & Mateo, 2010). Dur and Mateo (2010) propose that these strategies should be differentiated based on "hard" and "soft" bargaining, raising some concerns about the integrative and distributive typology. Namely, that distinguishing between integrative and distributive strategies is dependent, in part, on the intention of parties to come to an agreement that is most beneficial for themselves or one that creates the 'best' collective outcome. Classifying strategies based on how conflictive the tactics are simplifies characterization and reduces inconsistencies between empirical studies (Dur & Mateo, 2010).

Research suggests that weaker states should opt for soft bargaining techniques (Dur & Mateo, 2010). Weak actors have little to benefit from fronting an aggressive strategy and can instead lead to a loss of credibility and elicit a more aggressive response from the more powerful actor (Dur & Mateo, 2010). Essentially, weak parties should ingratiate themselves (Pruitt, 1983). Weaker parties should avoid taking strong, inflexible public commitments (Dur & Mateo, 2010). Entering negotiations with demands that are a far stretch from realistic outcomes is a very aggressive tactic that can increase concession costs and damage reputation (Dur & Mateo, 2010). However, weaker parties can opt for a more aggressive approach by forming a defensive coalition to deter compromise (Dur & Mateo, 2010). This technique signals to the other party that there is a threat of harm if they fail to comply (Dur & Mateo, 2010). Coalition makes these threats more credible (Dur & Mateo, 2010).

To save face, later in negotiations where the bargaining range shifts in favour of the other party, conciliatory statements can help reduce reputation damage (Dur & Mateo, 2010). Weaker parties can benefit from soft bargaining tactics, such as the signalling of flexibility (Dur & Mateo, 2010). Assuming this position from the start highlights to the other party that there is a common interest (Dur & Mateo, 2010). In multilateral bargaining situations, parties can make joint or lone proposals for compromise (Dur & Mateo, 2010-563). This can involve pushing a new proposal or altering existing proposals (Dur & Mateo, 2010). Parties who have more to lose if the negotiations do not lead to an agreement, typically the weaker actor, should opt for soft bargaining tactics to increase the probability of reaching agreement (Dur & Mateo, 2010).

Panke (2016) conducted a meta-analysis of over 500 negotiations with 27 international organisations assessed the dynamics of international negotiations and state participation. The study observed that a state's participation in negotiations signals their interests and power in negotiations. Prolonged silence by state actors in international issues can damage international regimes and diminish their bargaining power. States that were more vocal scored higher in their motivation and opportunity structures. Additionally, countries that had an established system for developing negotiation strategies, national positions and deploying diplomats were found to be more active in negotiations. Participation in regional groups also increased vocality, as explained by the ability to voice collective positions and better engage at an international level. State participation is often restricted by international regimes. The greater the number of states involved the more unwritten and formal rules in place. Thus, states tend to be more vocal in smaller regimes. As discussed, smaller states can benefit from membership with international organisations and regimes. However, this is often a burden to more powerful states. While equal participation in international regimes would increase the legitimacy of bargaining outcomes, it is limited by efficiency. Allowing weaker parties to participate equally would slow negotiations and create costly delays (Panke, 2016).

Considerations that go into choosing a dominant negotiation strategy extend beyond relative bargaining power (Dur & Mateo, 2010). Hard bargaining techniques can create long-term issues between parties by damaging relations and creating the potential for retaliation (Dur & Mateo, 2010). Distributive bargaining models encourage hard bargaining tactics which often involve unethical behaviour, puffery, and other deceptive behaviour (Kim, 2018). While players with less bargaining power have more to lose from deteriorated relations, the more powerful party can also suffer reputation damages and their relations with other countries not directly involved in negotiations (Dur & Mateo, 2010). To measure the effectiveness of bargaining strategies in international negotiations it is useful to look at the distribution of gains. Predictions for the distribution of gains within the bargaining zone and cooperation are key considerations in bargaining theory (Janusch, 2018). Generally, the greater the ZOPA, the more likely players are to cooperate (Kim, 2018). Evidently, with more players, the bargaining zone is decreased with greater programmatic distance between players (Kim, 2018). The distribution of gains is largely dependent upon the parties' audience costs, reputation for resolution and credibility (Janusch, 2018). A good reputation for resolving bargaining situations allows for better predictions of future behaviour honouring agreements and increases a party's bargaining power in negotiations. Audience costs are the costs to research, formulate and broadcast bargaining positions domestically (Kim, 2018).

Loopholes in distributional bargaining frameworks allow for power politics. Literature differentiates between de facto and de jure distribution (Schneider, 2011). De facto distribution arises when weaker states are essentially bought out (Schneider, 2011). International regimes often require unilateral agreement, and delays are disproportionately costly to larger state actors. Thus, it is often beneficial for larger state actors to "buy out" weaker actors then deliberate to achieve a better "side-deal" (Schneider, 2011). Weaker parties can benefit from threats to delay negotiations thereby manipulating their bargaining power. Distributional conflict increases when there is competition for resources that are limited (Schneider, 2011). Threats must be Pareto-efficient long term to hold any substantive credibility (Schneider, 2011). Promises, for example, that future governments are bound to will hold more weight in negotiations and increase the credibility of the bargaining party.

Crisis bargaining, describes a bargaining situation in which war is a possible outcome (Kydd & McManus, 2017). Kydd and McManus (2017) describe how bargaining in these situations differs from other bargaining situations. In crisis bargaining both assurances and threats can be used by negotiating parties to advance their position. Threats are best used to enforce bottom line positions in bargaining but should be used with caution. Threats can increase the likelihood of war. Assurances, on the other hand, will increase the likelihood of peaceful outcomes but can result in a weaker bargaining position. Threats are therefore generally more useful in bargaining strategies. However, where the goal is to alter the status quo, assurance strategies are ideal. The ideal strategy for crisis bargaining therefore must consider the trade-offs between threats and assurances (Kydd & McManus, 2017).

Moving away from the social psychology approach to explain bargaining in international negotiations, this section will explore the application of bargaining theory to international negotiations. This more formal approach also intersects with political science and economics. The forecasted equilibrium feature of the Nash Bargaining Solution is uniquely apt for international negotiations (Schneider, 2005). While traditionally applied to bilateral negotiations, the Nash Bargaining Solution can also predict outcomes in multilateral negotiations. Without going into the mathematics of the Nash Bargaining Solution, there is an assumption that the negotiating actors are aware of relative power differences and the bargaining goals of each actor. This axiomatic approach assumes that each party will only negotiate where there is the potential for utility or resource gains (Schneider, 2005). Schneider (2005) used the Nash Bargaining Strategy to predict bargaining power in international negotiations. He proposed that the Nash Bargaining Solution can analytically model the influence of causal mechanisms and imbalance in state capabilities that influence international negotiations. The baseline model assumes that no actor would negotiate without the possibility of gain, and therefore are Pareto superior. The predicted outcome is dependent upon the utility difference between parties and assumes that both actors are aware of the other parties desired outcome and will fully utilise their available resources. The Nash Bargaining Solution does not allow states to assess how their plays in negotiation could result in inefficient outcomes. It can, however, be a useful tool for forecasting the relative bargaining power of parties and credibility of commitments.

He further expands the Nash Bargaining Solution, in the context of international negotiations, which he calls the "realist" model. Under this model, the economic power of the state is considered. He predicted that the greater importance the state attaches to the desired outcome, the less likely they are to succeed (Schneider, 2005).

Schneider (2005) further discusses the applicability of the Nash Bargaining Solution and its limitations in international negotiation regimes. In negotiations, similar to the ZOPA, the bargaining space can be represented in a triangle configuration with both extremes, that is that one actor gets all and the other gets nothing and vice versa. The line that connects these two extremes is the Pareto frontier with the origin being the point at which the sum of disagreement points equates to zero. This is the point at which both players would accept any bargaining outcome that is Pareto beneficial. The Nash Bargaining Solution allows for the prediction of a unique bargaining outcome within the Pareto frontier. Where, for example, one party has a better relative BATNA, they will have more bargaining power, and thus shift their disagreement point on the Pareto frontier. The Nash Bargaining Solution will thus predict the distribution of gains in favour of the bargaining party with the highest BATNA. The Nash Bargaining Solution can also incorporate the law-based approach to international negotiations. Where for example, a party's position conflicts with international or domestic norms, the party loses credibility, and therefore bargaining power. Essentially, wherever the axioms in the Nash Bargaining Solution can be attributed to the relative bargaining power of parties the model can predict the outcome and probability of bargaining success (Schneider, 2005).

Different facets of negotiations are harder to frame analytically, and the Nash Bargaining Solution, used in isolation for establishing bargaining strategies in international negotiations would be inadvisable. International negotiations have the potential to carry significant consequences. As discussed, smaller state actors can utilise a number of strategies including manipulation of threat potential, law-based approaches to negotiation, reliance on non-governmental organisations and cooperation with other states to leverage their positions. Further, the Nash Bargaining Solution and other game theory frameworks can assist with framing strategies and to better predict bargaining outcomes. This is especially crucial for smaller states, whose bargaining strategy rely heavily on their ability for proper resource allocation. Allowing smaller states to participate effectively in international negotiations engenders better decision making processes and greater representation in the international regime.

References

Barry, B. (1980). Is it better to be powerful or lucky?. Political Studies, 28(2), 183-194.

Capacity and Concessions: Bargaining Power in Multilateral Negotiations

Drahos, P. (2003). When the weak bargain with the strong: negotiations in the World Trade Organization. International Negotiation, 8(1), 79-109.

Janusch, H. (2018). The interaction effects of bargaining power: The interplay between veto power, asymmetric interdependence, reputation, and audience costs. Negotiation Journal, 34(3), 219-241.

Kydd, A. H., & McManus, R. W. (2017). Threats and assurances in crisis bargaining. Journal of conflict resolution, 61(2), 325-348.

Panke, D. (2012). Dwarfs in international negotiations: how small states make their voices heard. Cambridge Review of International Affairs, 25(3), 313-328.

Panke, D. (2014). Is Bigger Better? Activity and Success in Negotiations in the United Nations General Assembly. Negotiation Journal, 30(4), 367-392.

Panke, D. (2016). Small states in the European Union: coping with structural disadvantages. Routledge.

Pruitt, D. G. (1983). Strategic choice in negotiation. American Behavioral Scientist, 27(2), 167-194.

Putnam, R. D. (1988). Diplomacy and domestic politics: the logic of two-level games. International organization, 42(3), 427-460.

Rickli, J. M. (2008). European small states' military policies after the Cold War: from territorial to niche strategies. Cambridge review of international affairs, 21(3), 307-325.

Schneider, C. J. (2011). Weak states and institutionalized bargaining power in international organizations. International Studies Quarterly, 55(2), 331-355.

Schneider, G. (2005). Capacity and concessions: Bargaining power in multilateral negotiations. Millennium, 33(3), 665-689.

Steinberg, R. H. (2002). In the shadow of law or power? Consensus-based bargaining and outcomes in the GATT/WTO. International organization, 56(2), 339-374.

Chapter 7: Political Persuasion and Social Control

Social, political, and military institutions use persuasive and influential methods to control various dimensions of individual and societal behaviour. The essence of human nature is social connection, without which we cannot function. Persuasion is essential to human behaviour as it is a step toward spreading knowledge and understanding. Leaders can convince thousands that their intentions are good. At the same time, mass manipulation is undeniable when politics and business practices are analyzed. This chapter will discuss the dynamics of mass persuasions, such as in the case of political and social movements. Simons (1976) argues that persuasion is about winning beliefs; thus, news platforms, scientists, teachers and academic resources navigate within the same grey area. Persuasion as human social behaviour is a form of attempted influence that seeks to alter how others think, feel, or act, though it differs from other forms of influence.

Real persuasion does not cause suffering or hold someone against their will. Nor is it the exchange of money or other such material inducements for actions performed by the person being influenced. Nor is it pressure to conform to the group or the authority of the powerful. Instead, persuasion is particularly useful to those trying to influence a large group to suggest potentially more appealing alternatives. For instance, the classic flexed bicep, handkerchief Rosie the Riveter poster from World War II "We Can Do It," calling women to work in the defence industries between 1940 and 1945, is an example of propaganda with persuasive messages. During this time, the female workforce in the United States increased by 10% (History.com Editors, 2010). Today, Rosie is a symbol of feminism to many. At the same time, the framing is an outstanding example of how the goals of the political elite can influence individual aspirations.

Female labour was necessary for the economy to function, and coercion was an option. A government will function much more smoothly with a consenting population. On the other hand, an example of coercion is exemplified by the history of military drafts where young people are "asked" to participate in combat with the alternative prison. Simons (1976) depicts persuasion as "human communication designed to influence the autonomous judgments and actions of others" (p.7). By working to persuade and convince those with a doctorate or in a government role leverage, credibility is granted to them by education and political prowess. There is a sentiment that individuals who occupy places of power are incapable of personal bias. Simons (1976) refers to it as "the guise of objectivity." Therefore it is unsurprising that history has a record of politicians, royal families and military leaders twisting the narrative to distract the masses from various nefarious actions. Undeniably, authority figures are human, and with access to power, they are capable of selfish behaviour for personal gain.

Nevertheless, political institutions thrive on the support of the people. A strong political leader or party can persuade the population to follow with absolute loyalty. In general, persuasion is an attempt to change someone's mind, feelings, or actions. Hence, the general understanding is that the government does not aim to persuade. Instead, democracy and monarchy rule with the consent of the citizens. In other words, a government must have a population willing to follow. Regardless, the social dynamics of any given society will impact how societies perceive a situation. Feld (1958) explains the dynamics of political persuasion in bureaucracy and policy. He posits that the audience in an instructive situation will consider the instructor superior and be prepared to consider further direction. Instead, in persuasive exchanges, the audience will typically view the speaker as an equal and consider the statements against personal experiences and insights (p. 79). Political dealings are not necessarily emotion driven—instead, elements of bureaucracy and social connection from the political process.

Persuasiveness in bureaucracy is typically attributed to elements of objectivity and rationalities within the bureaucratic process.

In other words, the formal policy stressing the rules, following the chain of command and hierarchy is attributed to a successful public. However, political persuasiveness is more often rooted in emotional and personal impressions. According to Hovland et al. research (as cited by Feld, 1958) article on Political Policy and Persuasion, the subject is often received as objective and rational in an instructive situation. In a persuasive situation, the topic is received as subjective and emotional (p.79). In political persuasion, the distinction between rational and emotional information is vital. It can influence the formulation of entire political movements. While it may be assumed that political success results from objective, rational action, it is increasingly apparent that society is not fuelled by rational choice, particularly in the United States, where political and social leaders are historically filled with emotion when communicating with the public despite the perpetual societal norm for powerful males to display little emotion. There is an undeniable phenomenon in which the passion of powerful men is a good display of emotion, mainly when speaking about freedom.

There are varying arguments about the degree to which political leaders aim to persuade the masses. Nevertheless, with increased access to media and communication, speakers have multiple persuasion points of access. Studies of individual attitudes change how people are prone to change their stated beliefs in response to persuasive arguments or even the mere knowledge that others hold a specific opinion (Nowak, Szamrej & Latané, p. 363, 1990). Attitude is a complex psychological concept anchored in elements of individual evaluation. Bristol, Petty, and Guyer 92019) discuss in A Historical View on Attitudes and Persuasion the research foundation for contemporary studies of persuasion and attitude.

While political figures may use manipulation tactics to get votes, theory tells us politics can not function without the people's consent. Instead, Feld (1958) explains that all stable governments maintain an underlying set of formulaic expressions subject to automatic obedience...and machinery for disseminating throughout the governed." The formulaic expressions are the judgments demonstrated by the political elite solidifying the class distinction between the political class and the remaining population. In other words, expressions are the laws and policies the governing bodies implement. However, political leaders must conform to the dominant or near dominant formal and informal norms of society to succeed to any degree in western politics.

There is a tendency for the public to treat government action in the form of policy as a reflection of societal needs rather than a "political instrument" (Feld, 1958, p. 83). In reality, the public has very little insight into the motivation for policy change. Propaganda is readily incorporated into politics in the form of essential information. Propaganda describes the systemic dissemination of information, particularly biased or misleading, to promote a political cause or point of view. Typically through some form of media in contemporary societies (OED, 2022). Pier Paolo Pedrini (2017), author of Propaganda, Persuasion and the Great War: Heredity in the Modern Sale of Products and Political Ideas, explains that psychology suggests a group does not have the same psychological characteristics as an individual. Instead, a group or "herd" of people requires behaviour instruction. In other words, the collective consciousness does not   have thoughts. Impulses and habits drive it. One of these impulses is to follow a trusted leader (p. 58). The idea that the human herd is driven to follow a leader suggests there is little need for persuasion. Instead, the herd will default to follow; thus, persuasion becomes pertinent when psychology, manipulation, coercion and greed become involved in the political process. Pedrini is entirely accurate in that being in a group alters human behaviour. Bristol, Petty, and Guyer discuss the research on the impact of others on a person's susceptibility to influence, which is measured by the development of attitude measurement scales (p. 7). Notable research from the early 1900s on attitude change and persuasion found attitudes can change from explanation and attempting to convince. Further, research conducted by Sherif (1936) on societal norms found that people turn to others in ambiguous situations. In other words, if the social expectations are unclear, people turn to others, particularly those in positions of authority or with the loudest voice. By the mid-1940s, the critical theme in persuasion was the role classical conditioning

CHAPTER 7: POLITICAL PERSUASION AND SOCIAL CONTROL

and cognitive psychology could be applied to the study of attitude change. Today, research on attitudes and persuasion continues to capture the attention of social psychologists. Most of the attention is placed on the phenomena of "self-persuasion," which is the self-generated arguments created to convince others of the unintentional influence of one's evaluation of the topic. For example, Brinol et al. (2012) found that individuals who had doubts about their stance on a particular topic would subconsciously attempt to create a persuasive message, leading to increased self-persuasion. P. 17).

Psychology is relevant in the conversation of persuasion as psychological data about persuasion, propaganda and government advance. It is undeniable that the powerful will access and utilize this information to influence. At the same time, there is little to be definitively concluded in terms of intention when discussing government rulings. The influence is also undeniable. Feld (1958) argues that the critical distinguishing factor in successful political persuasion is the degree to which the leaders' decisions are implemented. In other words, a speaker will not persuade a group if there is no significant change to policy and practice. Thus, in a genuinely democratic society, blind obedience does not exist. All choices are subject to public scrutiny and the democratic processes. In stark contrast is pure despotism, wherein the ruler may change laws on a personal whim. Political persuasion is demonstrated through covert and overt means. Such as subtle suggestions or blatant adverts. Overt government manipulation is not at all widespread. Instead, covert manipulation is historically recorded, and this experience has impacted the collective conscious trust in government. The lack of trust in government can contribute to political and social unrest, possibly increasing crime rates. Similar to political propaganda, disinformation is the modern term for disseminating deliberately false information. Disinformation is particularly harmful when supplied by a government or its agent to a foreign power or the media to influence the policies or opinions of those who receive it (OED, 2022).

Simons (1976) outlines political persuasion through the Republican party's influence on the Presidential leaders Nixon and Reagan (p.

244). The United States Republican party is a fantastic example of the overt use of persuasion. Political campaigning in the United States is known to maximize the "art of persuasion," with campaign managers specializing in speech writing and booking photo opportunities to create a public image essential for a successful political career in the American political climate. Polticitican worldwide has adopted the American "new politics," characterized by neverending campaigning (p. 245). In other words, the act of campaigning was a short-term time of political persuasion characterized by speeches and celebration. While there is a socially defined campaign period in modern society, successful candidates typically hold status before entering the race. Moreover, candidacy requires endorsements from influential organizations to hold any credibility. Thus, persuasion seems to be a critical piece of the American political process.

Influence and power are principles of social control. Scholars of power and influence study social control as patterns of enforcement by powerful institutions and groups through which society maintains social order and cohesion. Social control is enacted on an institutional and individual level; however, it is typically a response to deviant, problematic, threatening or undesirable behaviour (Carmichael, 2012). Research from Smith & Fink (2019) on Understanding the Influential People and Social Structures Shaping Compliance is an inspection of persuasion. The study comprised 195 adults and accessed two research paths: influential people and the social context they attempt to influence. Smith & Fink (2019) found that individual attributes can influence potential network-based power and the network-based predictability of compliance. The participants were shown a sociogram of 11 people connected by friendships. Participants were asked to imagine themselves in this group, identify a position, select another member for interaction, and predict their likelihood of complying with the member's request.

Nowak et al. (1990) explain that individuals in one social context behave may differently than they would outside that context. A relationship between individuals and their social context can result in the emergence of new norms at the individual and societal levels. These new norms are not a result of laws. Moreover, the patterns of social behaviour that are typical of the group may shift. The shift in social behaviour is relevant in the context of persuasion in politics because as a political belief increases in popularity, there will become a shift in societal norms. A shift in societal norms can occur when politically influential public figures are prone to twist a narrative to conform to disinformation. Nowak et al. (1900) argue that "laws operating on lower levels of social reality may have unforeseen, seemingly emergent, consequences for higher levels, which, in turn, will affect the social environment facing lower level units" (p. 362). Lower levels of social reality can be understood as the lower social and economic classes. The critical study of society takes a hard look at the elite's role in forming laws and criminalizing the remaining population. Specifically, laws and policies limiting the ability of the "lower levels" of society to participate can increase visible crime. The question of whether the mainstream public would prefer to simply not look at the members of society that are struggling is answered by the increased movement of people to the suburbs and how the western world places the sick and seniors away in lonely places unless a high economic status is involved. In addition to institutionalizing the sick and elderly, the "deviant" or criminal are institutionalized. The need for a space to contain specific parts of the population is a twisted human behaviour. However, we accept the control over specific groups. These groups are individuals that seem to deviate from what is socially acceptable. Therefore, when the hidden population increases in visibility, there can be a negative response from those of a higher socioeconomic status. The social stigma toward criminals and destitution is undeniable throughout society, and the phenomenon is not entirely the elite's responsibility. Though, the elite are willing participants in the marginalization by allowing the process to continue.

Notably, governing bodies negotiate with the public through elections and open parliament. Though, the marginalized populations are not nearly as capable of participating in the political process or presenting themselves in open parliament as the privilege. For the political process to succeed, there must be an interaction between the politicians and the voters. The political process must succeed because the government does not want a rogue population. As mentioned, a large group requires control. Despite the individual ability for intelligence, there appears to be a historical inability for the masses to function with moral and societal order.

Opposing governing forces may create an illusion of choice as governing is inevitable. For the interaction to function smoothly, there must be persuasion and negotiation. Social science suggests that contemporary politics requires the people's consent to function as the democratic process. The interaction can be made up of a potential political leader or policy maker offer. The population may accept the new "norm" with votes or respond with protests or lobbying. However, a notable element of this process is the dominant process by which norms are created. This process was created and is controlled by the dominant population. The phenomenon of social control originates from a socially influential or powerful individual or group. Social control is the "control of a person or group by wider society to enforce social norms, through socialization, policing, laws, or similar measures" (OED, 2022). Social control research focuses on the powerful forces influencing public perception. While a gross oversimplification, this dynamic stretches beyond the political process into social processes such as the fashion industry, religion, education and beyond. The choices of the ruling classes are deeply impactful on the population at large. While persuasiveness is simply a means to an end, there are implications for the individual. Not exclusively in terms of policy, but rather, the social environment can influence individuals. The study of social control is a broad subfield of sociology that involves criminologists, political sociologists, and those interested in the sociology of law and punishment, as well as scholars from a variety of disciplines, including philosophy, anthropology, political science, economics, and law" (Carmichael, 2012). The subfield includes both macro and micro components. In other words, social control is easily separated into societal and individual levels.

Social control at a societal level focuses on the institutional goals and mechanisms of social society, such as police, law, and punishment

(Carmichael, 2012). Today, political institutions attempt to control and negotiate by subtle acts of control. The ruling class has gone so far as to utilize modern technology and surveillance to persuade. In the past, militarized institutions such as the police force, fire department and any form of army, military, marines and private schools across Canada and the United States were rigid in the policy. Elements of persuasion and negotiation were not encouraged as there is a seemingly "shoot first, as questions later" dynamic in military institutions. At the same time, gun violence is not a constant among all militarized institutions. Today, governing is less focused on political goals. The United States is an example of a group behaving disorganizedly, removing them from the category of those who must be persuaded to those who must be controlled. Historically, corporeal punishment, torture and solitary confinement were methods to persuade the public, whether the children at home or the inmate in the cell, to cooperate and fall in line. Control by force is not nearly as acceptable as it once was, so there is a push toward more tactical means to sway the public.

Religious institutions go through great strides to spread the gospel or whatever else as an attempt to persuade nonbelievers. The tactics include an afterlife with all our wildest dreams, no expenses, all of our loved ones, and the approval of an omnipotent being. The persuasiveness of this afterlife is undeniably persuasive. Further, the social status assigned to priests, fathers, and the pope represents the degree to which powerful institutions will elevate one individual in an attempt to control. This feeds back to the discussion above about the informative versus the persuasive dialogues with powerful speakers. In religious ceremonies, the speaker speaks from experience, knowledge and spirituality. The aim is undeniable to "spread the word" rather than to share the truth. . The mechanisms of social control prevalent in contemporary society thrive on elements of persuasion and influence. Jespersen et al. (2007) in Surveillance, Persuasion and Panopticon discuss the increasing interest in monitoring ordinary folks' daily activities. The Panopticon is the original name for a prison designed to create the illusion of constant surveillance. The design consists of a lone tower looming in the center of the institutions with stacked rings of cells with nothing but bars. The guard tower created the illusion of constant surveillance by limiting the inmate's ability to see into the tower, thereby creating no way to observe the authority. Thus, prisoners were persuaded to participate by the possibility of being caught. This phenomenon is increasingly relevant in contemporary society with dash cameras and stop-light cameras; there is little that one can do without video recording

Nevertheless, Jespersen et al. (2007) concluded that surveillance makes it possible to change someone's behaviour if they are aware they are being watched (p. 119). In other words, institutions use overt social control to police and covert methods to gather data to frame persuasive statements and maximize results effectively. Scholars interested in the macro aspects of social control examine questions related to the role of elites, the state, and other political and religious institutions in establishing the norms and rules people are governed by. Whereas the micro elements of social control tend to focus more on the role that socialization and peer influence have in limiting human action. (Carmichael, 2012). Religious institutions and persuasion in intimate interactions are significant as faith-based groups are culturally widespread. Further, the connection one has with their faith is emotional. Political and religious institutions are groups accessing formal means of social control. The justice system is an undeniable means of social control that creates the illusion of choice while dominated by persuasion. The negotiation tactics revolve around balancing what is acceptable to the masses and the dominant class's requirements. Religious institutions, on the other hand, present as inviting. Religion is not persuasive because there is an inherent appeal. Instead, there is the threat of damnation used in collaboration with songs and rituals. Nevertheless, the community and closeness are appealing. An informal look at the negotiation and persuasion process is the power of the media in the political process and the behaviour of the public. Research has suggested that surveillance may influence the behaviour of social groups, especially if the results of the surveillance studies are communicated using mass media (Jespersen et al., 2007, p. 119). Thus, influence and persuasion are natural tools in the era of media marketing. With the help of attitude and persuasion research, corporations can control the buying power of the masses.

References

Briñol, P., Petty, R. E., & Guyer, J. J. (2019). A historical view on attitudes and persuasion. In Oxford Research Encyclopedia of Psychology.

Burkley E., Hatvany T. (2016). Self Control and The Susceptibility to Persuasion, Compliance and Conformity. The Psychology of Consumer and Social Influence: Theory and Research. Nova Science Publishers, Inc, 30-41. ISBN: 978-1-63485-498-6

Carmichael J. (2012). Social Control. obo in Sociology. doi: 10.1093/obo/9780199756384-0048

Cialdini, R. B., & Goldstein, N. J. (2004). Social influence: Compliance and conformity. Annual review of psychology, 55(1), 591-621.

Feld, M. D. (1958). Political Policy and Persuasion: The Role of Communications from Political Leaders. The Journal of Conflict Resolution, 2(1), 78–89. http://www.jstor.org/stable/172847

History.com Editors. 2021. Rosie the Riveter. History. A&E Television Networks. https://www.history.com/topics/world-war-ii/rosie-the-riveter.

Knowles E. S. , & Linn J. A. (2004). Resistance and Persuasion. Psychology Press. Jespersen, J. L., Albrechtslund, A., Øhrstrøm, P., Hasle., P. F. V., & Albretsen, J. (2007). Surveillance, Persuasion, and Panopticon. In Y. de Kort, W. IJsselsteijn, C. Midden, B. E., & B. J. Fogg (Eds.), Persuasive Technology: Second International Conference on Persuasive Technology, PERSUASIVE 2007 : Revised Selected Papers (pp. 109-120). IEEE Computer Society Press. Lecture Notes in Computer Science Vol.4744/2007

Maslow, A., & Lewis, K. J. (1987). Maslow's hierarchy of needs. Salenger Incorporated, 14(17), 987-990.

Nowak, A., Szamrej, J., & Latané, B. (1990). "From private attitude to public opinion: A dynamic theory of social impact." Psychological Review 97, 362–376. doi:10.1037//0033-295X.97.3.362

OED Online. 2022. Propaganda. Oxford University Press, June 2022. Web. 6 August 2022. OED Online. 2022. Social Control. Oxford University Press. www.oed.com/view/Entry/183739

Sherif, M. (1936). The psychology of social norms. Harper. Simons, H. W. (1976). Persuasion in Society. Reading: Addison-Wesley, 21. Chicago

Smith, R. A., & Fink, E. L. (2019). Understanding the influential people and social structures shaping compliance. Journal of Social Structure, 16(1).

Chapter 8: Marketing, Persuasion, and Influence

Psychology, along with a wide range of other academic disciplines, has influenced consumer behaviour and marketing research. The global economic structure has set forth a system designed to predict and meet individual consumers' desires. However, To conform is to follow the expected socially constructed standard of behaviour. In other words, individuals are expected to behave according to a societal standard. At the same time, the idea of conformity may trigger thoughts of mindless drones following the leader without question. Conformity is encouraged through education, religion and mass communication platforms. Conformity is a form of social influence maximized with persuasive messages. Conformity is essential in the marketing industry as the sales of goods in large quantities is where the money can be found. Influence, persuasion and conformity are tools of the current marketing industry, and all are found to manipulate the consumer. This chapter will discuss social influence through marketing persuasion—the role of conformity in manipulating the current consumer market. Further, a discussion of how social behaviour is exploited for marketing and increased consumption results from manipulative marketing tactics to persuade consumers.

Media often creates an image of desire and scarcity in the images. Marketing campaigns with striking images of an attractive individual consuming a beverage or driving a fancy sports car can suggest to viewers that the vehicle or beverage contributes to the overall appeal. While in reality, the marketing campaign is specifically designed to appeal to the inherent human sense of belonging that is often accompanied by sex appeal. The global marketplace is designed for the individual on a global scale. Thus, the appeal of marketing to the individual is arguably the empathetic, unique and ethical face of modern corporations. While marketing campaigns are specifically designed to appeal to consumers and attract massive numbers of buyers. Further, any change in behaviour to match that of others is referred to as conformity and such behaviour is often dictated by social norms (Cialdini and Goldstein, 2004). Therefore, marketing industries press the consumer to make a change in behaviour by purchasing the product or following the trend.

The inherent human need to belong is the idea that people have a fundamental drive to be accepted, whether in relationships with others or by participating in a social group. There is psychological research to support the human drive for belonging. The psychology of belongingness is not new. Relatively well-known psychologists acknowledge the importance of primarily positive, meaningful relationships. Notably, Baumeister & Leary (1995) explain that the contention that people are motivated to create and maintain interpersonal bonds is not novel. Psychologist Maslow & Lewis (1987) stresses the importance of belonging in the hierarchy of needs theory, which places love and belonging in the middle of the five components required for a human to function to its maximum potential and reach self-actualization. According to the hierarchy of needs, physiological needs create the base of what is commonly referred to as the "Pyramid of Needs," with the foundation being the need for air, water, food, shelter, clothing and sleep. Following a foundation made up of what is required for basic survival is the need for safety—followed by the need for love and belonging, self-esteem and self-actualization. Self-actualization is when a human animal can move past the phase of basic survival and experience self-acceptance, experience a deeper purpose in life, and potentially experience their meaning in life. Most importantly, this is when an individual can maximize their potential, essentially living life to the fullest. In contrast, the hierarchy of needs does present a neat equation for human happiness. Marketing industries appeal to the need for human belonging by suggesting that products and practices are essential for belonging.

\Marketing persuasion is overt and covertly spread, with advertising agencies seemingly aiming to penetrate the subconscious. Unsurprisingly, research suggests psychological techniques are commonplace in marketing and consumerism (Baryshnikova, 2017). Such behaviour is modelled by media personalities and encouraged through scientifically designed methods to exploit the inherent human need to belong. Moreover, advancements in technology allow algorithms to collect data with every click. As mentioned in previous chapters on political persuasion and social control, surveillance is a critical element of contemporary persuasion. Increased access to individual data allows marketers to access data otherwise inaccessible. (Jespersen et al., 2007). Markedly, persuasive marketing through emotional appeal is an effective tool allowing corporations to access the wealth of a demographic. The persuasion tactics utilized by modern marketing result from a great deal of scientific research.

Feld (1958) stresses that political candidates' dedication to marketing in the form of advertisements and speech writing are efforts to maintain contact with the public to manipulate, reassure and control while in office. There is a great deal of distrust regarding political candidates spreading "fake news." In addition to concerns surrounding political parties focusing on goals that are not in the constituents' best interest. Instead, persuasive methods are used to manipulate voters into conforming to the political elite's ideology while overlooking the masses' desires. The political dynamic where politicians access media platforms to persuade the public of disinformation creates distrust in political leaders. Further, politicians have access to social media platforms, allowing the persuasion to move past the television screen to a much more personal exchange. While the social disconnect remains the same, individuals may feel more connected to politicians and other influential individuals when following them on social media platforms. In other words, the media has created new access to individuals who have the power to persuade. Rather than waiting to observe a powerful speaker in the village square or on the morning news. Viewers can simply touch the screen and follow the opinions of literally anyone with access to the internet and a social media account.

The persuasiveness of the internet is a magnificent method to share profound facts about important world events. However, the internet is not the place for honest dialogue. Instead, social platforms are a source of complete transparency or complete anonymity. Social media influencers make up a small number of the internet while being able to persuade the masses. Media communication is a direct means of persuading an audience of a particular intention or the quality of an item.

The manipulation through advertising became an issue with the rise of the media and consumer relationships. Danicu (2014) suggests that as media, advertisements and consumption intertwined, shifting from the mission of marketing to that of meeting the needs of customers. Instead, marketers began to appeal to power dynamics between the company and the consumer. Nevertheless, research seems to suggest that people rely on the opinions of friends and family and market persuasion has little impact on an individual's desire to buy a product. Baryshnikova (2017) supports that "despite how refined marketing campaigns are, the most important thing to generate success is to make people talk about the product and recommend it to others" (p. 33). In other words, a marketing campaign will never be as good as word of mouth, predominantly positive conversations about services. There is a population known as Social media influencers (SMIs) who represent new types of marketing independent of large-scale marketing campaigns. Freberg et al., 2010) outline the SMI as a new independent third-party endorser who influences view attitudes through their media platform. SMI uses tweets, blogs, and various modes of posting to share opinions and insight into products and social events.

Freberg et al. (2010) research have a limited sample (n=4). Nevertheless, a proposed finding is the transparency of SMI, a potential appeal as a marketing source compared to the company's CEO. This is to say, the media communications of the SMIis perceived as more honest. Particularly as many SMI participate in unboxing or product reviews. Corporations send SMI items to review at a discount cost in this situation. In contrast, influencers can purchase the items with personal funds. Either way, SMI will record a review of the product. After which, the influencers' opinions can impact the success of whatever is being sold. In other words, a product's success can be heavily attributed to whether an SMI supports or "cancels" the brand. Cancelling is a social phenomenon where SMI uses a platform to influence an entire population's attitudes to remove a product, person, brand or behaviour from the sphere of acceptable social norms.

While cancelling is not always an overt practice, there are situations where SMI calls followers to bombard and harass the target of what is known as "cancel culture." Conformity and persuasion are essentially the foundation of "cancel culture," as there is an unspoken bond to confirm. The sense of community surrounding an SMI significantly influences various forms of marketing in contemporary society. There is a massive amount of intentionality in creating marketing campaigns. Individuals work tirelessly, intending to go viral.

Moreover, social media marketing is an industry that works with influencers to maximize viewers and, therefore, persuasiveness. Persuasion in social media is distinct from the newspaper or television in that the personal opinions of the SMIs are unedited. The dynamics created allow for candid human expression that can be a fantastic opportunity for shared experiences and destigmatization. However, with the good must come the bad. In other words, some individuals access social media platforms with malicious intentions. Alternatively, possibly worse are people who take advantage of social media platforms and speak from a place of ignorance.

Ignorance and persuasion are not social phenomena that should co-inside—in other words, giving access to the media and creating a space for all people to speak. What has also occurred is a population of individuals who cannot process the truth.

Thus, rather than pivoting in the standard practices in the form of conformity. These individuals look for outside explanations for unexpected or unexplainable experiences. Thus, persuasion and conformity must be understood to succeed in the marketing and consumption industries. A constant stream of subtle advertisements bombards modern individuals. In comparison, the number of persuasive messages absorbed by the average person in an industrialized society is debatable. Studies conducted by advertising companies suggest that the average American is exposed to thousands of daily ads (Forbes, 2017). Modern media marketing takes many forms, including a persuasive copy in online advertising. Persuasive copywriting aims to create an emotional impact or interest in the product. Thus, media is marked by mass communication. As a tool of influence, print, television, movies, video games, music, mobile phones, and the internet are means of modern communication and a vessel for persuasive messages. As some suggest, any attempt to change a person's mind or attitude can be understood as persuasion (Petty and Briñol, 2010).

An innate psychological compulsion for belonging is considered a motivation for human behaviour. The psychology of behaviourism has influenced consumer and marketing research (Wells, 2014). Like what? Moreover, several studies support the idea that impaired self-control increases people's tendencies to conform to the behaviour of those around them. (What studies?). Self-control depletion increases susceptibility to conformity. Mainly self-control depletion occurs when one conforms to descriptive norms. Descriptive norms are the perceptions of how people behave in reality, whereas an injunctive norm refers to people's attitudes about how others should behave (Burkley & Hatvany, 2017, p. 37).

Media communications are not necessarily clearly portrayed. Instead, marketing persuasion of the modern era is both subtle and brazen. In other words, marketing agencies use covert and overt means to manipulate the consumer. Specifically, product placement and "subliminal messaging" are used to attract consumer attention. While subliminal messaging is not a typical tool used to manipulate consumerism, the phenomenon created the idea that media corporations are willing to spread marketing campaigns without consumer consent. Thus, the tactics marketing industries use to persuade the consumer are relevant. At the same time, Danciu (2014) argues that persuasion and manipulation of the consumer through advertising is standard practice. There are elements of marketing and influence with an appearance of persuasion with manipulative tactics. Marketing that is non-manipulative is informative and persuasive. Non-manipulative marketing aims to provide clear, logical and truthful insight into a product. The driving forces are the facts and appealing to the consumer's emotion. By contrast, manipulative marketing implies facts with minimal ethical standards. Danciu (2014) contends that the marketing industry must conform to ethical standards rather than tunnel vision on maximizing customer happiness through manipulation. Moreover, marketing communication generally uses specific language to ease any concerns the consumer may have. Thus, despite manipulative tactics by marketing companies, the modern consumer is often first interested in the product and then in the corporation's ethics. Many manipulative advertisements are difficult to prove because of their controversial nature and content. Danciu (2014) continues that companies use the stimuli, the techniques and the mechanisms of advertising to manipulate the consumers.

By framing a product or an experience as necessary to the human experience, marketing agencies appeal to a scientifically backed human desire. Thus, the individual is not the core concern of mass marketing. Instead, marketing campaigns target a massive and diverse population simultaneously. From funeral homes to amusement parts, advertisements aim to demonstrate the fantastic qualities of a given item. Moreover, product marketing is a method of persuasion targetting all social classes and regions with ads varying in jargon and editing to appeal to a range of populations. Product placement is a marketing tactic that boldly displays goods in the shot that financially support the program. Thus, presenting the brand to the viewer increases sales and says, "we paid for this." It is difficult to overlook the soda or cereal box boldly displayed in the center of the screen, proudly consumed by the brave, attractive protagonist.

Several studies support the idea that impaired self-control increases people's tendencies to conform to the behaviour of those around them. Social science defines the perceptions of how people behave as descriptive norms, whereas an injunctive norm refers to attitudes about how others should behave (Burkley & Hatvany, 2017). Suppose self-control depletion inhibits the ability to resist social influences. Consequently, ongoing contact with a persuasive influence can make one more likely to conform to pressures. The depletion effect is an essential element of human social behaviour for various reasons. In marketing and persuasion, the theory that self-control is a limited resource suggests that the more an individual experiences ads, the more likely they are to make a purchase.

Therefore, corporations arguably take advantage of this psychological phenomenon through the constant and repetitive displays of modern marketing. With the current understanding of the depletion effect, researchers would be suited to research how the depletion effect can be reduced, overcome, or used to promote persuasion. Thus, contemporary marketing agencies and those studying the psychology of advertising examine resistance and individual attitudes toward product marketing—Burkley & Hatvany (2019) outline research that challenged participants with aggressively persuasive messages. The research was conducted where research participants were subjected to a series of persuasive instances followed by an assessment of the participants' regulatory system to determine whether the resistance was consuming. The findings suggest that social influences deplete people of self-control, leaving them vulnerable to performance impairments. Some will be more susceptible to persuasive messages, compliance techniques, and conformity pressures when attempting to persuade for prolonged periods. Simply, resisting persuasive messages reduces the capacity for self-control.

Moreover, there is research to demonstrate that self-control is a limited resource. Meaning that once it is expended, it leads to impaired performance on future self-control tasks. This "depletion effect" of self-control has been shown to impair people's ability to regulate their thoughts, feelings, and behaviours (Burkley & Hatvany, 2016). Attempts to test whether resisting conformity pressures consume self-control conducted by various researchers found the depletion effect to be a verifiable occurrence experienced by those subjected to repetitive interactions with conformity pressures. Examples of research on self-control depletion asked men and women to make a self- descriptive videotape in gender normative or counter-normative manner. In other words, women and men each were asked to record themselves behaving in what would be overtly feminine and masculine ways.

Next, participants' self-control resources were assessed using a physical regulation task: Holding a hand grip for as long as possible. The research found that the people who resisted the norms by acting outside the typical behaviour patterns showed decreased self-control. The decrease in self-control was recorded by a handgrip task, in which respondents were less persistent. Thus, going against the grain by actively resisting consumes self-control resources. A further study found that teenagers low in chronic trait self-control were more likely to conform to the normative behaviour of their peers, resulting in greater smoking and drinking. Self-control depletion increases susceptibility to conformity pressures (Burkley & Hatvany, 2017).

Although, conforming to societal norms may require individuals to overlook innate inherent and personal impulses. Overlooking inherits personal drives, thereby employing self-control resources to override immediate and self-interested impulses and according to the depletion effect, denying oneself an authentic life consumes self-control resources. Thus, the creation of modern ads has created an environment where the expectations to conform originated with the corporation interested in wealth. Specifically, advertisements are created by marketing firms hired by corporations trying to sell a demographic of goods or services. However, people do not want to feel they are being sold. Knowing this, marketing agencies and ruling institutions, like government security organizations, have found a way to access data to predict a consumer's potential needs.

Marketing industries have shifted the method of persuasion from retroactive advertising to proactive methods. Rather than showing everyone the same image, technology has allowed corporations to access data and curate the ads to appeal to the consumers' needs. Radhakrishnan (2013) defines data mining as the "exploration and analysis of large quantities of data to discover meaningful patterns and rules." However, data mining aims to "allow corporations to improve marketing, sales and customer support operations through better understanding customer needs" (p. 41). The surveillance and the collection of data are commonly referred to as data mining. In other words, data mining is extracting and discovering patterns in large-scale data sets involving complex statistics. Data mining allows businesses and marketing agencies to access customer data from a database powered by artificial intelligence. While data mining is not a malicious action, there is the potential for manipulation of consumers with the unlawful sale of data. Data mining aims to automate the processing of financial data to support companies in terms of future trends.

Indirect forms of marketing persuasion are of particular interest to social researchers. Self-persuasion encouraged consumers to create arguments about a product or behaviour rather than providing them with the argument (p. 1076). Advertising and self-persuasion theory suggests that consumers will aim to improve attitudes toward products, and advertisements support consumers in the process (Bernritter et al., 2017; Nagler, 2022). Internal forms of persuasion are significant in marketing as they reduce the possibility of the consumer showing apprehensiveness toward the marketing. In other words, internal persuasion increases the likelihood that a persuasive technique will succeed. Generally, arguments and information that appear to originate from oneself are considered more accurate and trustworthy, thereby making it much more persuasive than an external source.

Self-persuasion is an effective marketing technique as it does not require direct interaction with the consumer. Instead, formulating questions instead of statements will set the foundation for self-persuasion, as a marketing campaign asking "Why have you not XYZ '' will trigger the question within the viewer. Resaerch by Bernritter et al. (2017) conducted on self-persuasion and marketing tested tipping rates in undergraduate students recruited through an online University. The participants were asked to tip after imagining having lunch. The study aimed to test whether participants would tip more money after reading an article about why tipping is vital to servers. Findings showed that when participants were highly involved with tipping, self-persuasion was much more effective than the arguments provided. However, for low and moderate involvement participants, the effect of self-persuasion did not significantly differ. Therefore, the conclusion is that self-persuasion is a valuable technique in situations where consumers are highly involved with the target behaviour (p. 1083). In other words, the more relevant a product or situation is to a viewer or consumer, the more likely self-persuasion will be effective, resulting in successful marketing.

References

Baryshnikova, E. (2017). Persuasive techniques used in marketing and advertising based on psychological factors. European Journal of Marketing. ISSN: 0309-0566.

Baumeister, R. F., & Leary, M. R. (1995). The need to belong: desire for interpersonal attachments as a fundamental human motivation. Psychological bulletin, 117(3), 497–529.

Bernritter S.F., van Ooijen I., Müller C.N.B. (2017). Self-persuasion as marketing technique: the role of consumers' involvement

Danciu, V. (2014). Manipulative marketing: persuasion and manipulation of the consumer through advertising. Theoretical & Applied Economics, 21(2), 19–34.

Freberg, K., Graham, K., McGaughey, K., & Freberg, L. A. (2011). Who are the social media influencers? A study of public perceptions of personality. Public relations review, 37(1), 90-92.

Hill, S. J., Lo, J., Vavreck, L., & Zaller, J. (2013). How quickly we forget: The duration of persuasion effects from mass communication. Political Communication, 30(4), 521-547.

Joel E. Dimsdale. (2021). Dark Persuasion : A History of Brainwashing From Pavlov to Social Media. Yale University Press.

Radhakrishnan, B., Shineraj, G., & Anver Muhammed, K. M. (2013). Application of data mining in marketing. International Journal of Computer Science and Network, 2(5), 41-46

Shen, F., Sheer, V. C., & Li, R. (2015). Impact of narratives on persuasion in health communication: A meta-analysis. Journal of Advertising, 44(2), 105-113. Wells, V. K. (2014). Behavioural psychology, marketing and consumer behaviour: a literature review and future research agenda. Journal of Marketing Management, 30(11–12), 1119–1158. https://doi.or g/10.1080/0267257X.2014.929161

Chapter 9: Influence, Cults, and Conspiracies

Social movements influence nearly all facets of daily life and are commonly associated with progress. Yet, the change that stems from social movements is not entirely constructive nor consistently progressive. Social change is triggered by public health threats, as demonstrated by the AIDS epidemic and the COVID-19 pandemic. Further economic instability or limitations to social freedoms will initiate social change. During this, it is assumed that people respond with common sense, particularly in times of crisis. However, when faced with massive social change, some are not comforted by the messages offered by political leaders and popular media. As mentioned in previous chapters, the individual and the crowd do not share the same psychological profile. When faced with social, political or economic upheaval, the masses turn to authority for guidance (CITE). However, if the authority's message is not received, propaganda, conspiracy, and mass hysteria result in well-documented global phenomena (Jacobs, 1965; Stahl & Lebedun, M., 1974; Kirkpatrick, 1975). Mass hysteria is a shared panic often characterized by physical symptoms often triggered by shared stress and trauma. Speculations about society's norms and the legitimacy of "mainstream" communication sources can morph into social movements that influence social behaviour at the societal and individual levels.

Individuals with a general distrust for authority, lack community and are experiencing loneliness may look for an alternate data source if the information from the mainstream media does not align with their expectations or internalized social norms. It may be that the anonymity and community offered by online media forums and groups provide a space to share concerns about authority and speculate wildly. Perhaps the ability to share global crises and injustice through the media has created the sense that the world is in a constant state of chaos. Access to information exemplifying the reality of global news offers critical perspectives to otherwise ignorant populations. Then again, some struggle to comprehend the reality of novel global crises—individuals who cannot comprehend the natural cause of events. Conspiracy theories often attempt to explain the ultimate cause of events as a secret plot by influential organizations or individuals (Douglas & Sutton, 2008). Followers of undeniably irrational conspiracy theories may appear ignorant; even so, the change in belief is a result of legitimate experiences. And yet, internal and external influences that create and spread a conspiracy are often not considered.

While there is a common stereotype that conspiracy theories thrive in western cultures, there is little evidence supporting these stereotypes (van Prooijen and Douglas, 2017). Although, conspiracy theories are not increasingly common or inherently persuasive. Alternatively, conspiracy theories' are belief systems that attract individuals based on the content and qualities (Sternisko et al., 2020). Once blessed with the age of information, the global population is now in the age of disinformation. However, mass media and communication have created a phenomenal means to spread knowledge. Disinformation and the echo chamber often created by internet use can result in increased distrust in government and social movements.

Social science research has found a correlation between conspiracy theory beliefs and anti-democratic attitudes, prejudice and non-normative political behaviour (Sternisko et al., 2020). Democracy is essential to the smooth functioning of a capitalist western society. Violent social movements are often associated with conspiracy theories that threaten the mechanisms of society by denying the legitimacy of government information. Contradictory messages are powerful when there are weaknesses in society. Research suggests it is human nature to try to find an explanation when experiencing political, economic or social disturbances (van Prooijen & Douglas, 2017). Prooijen and Douglas (2017) focus on societal crises' role in individual and societal tendency to accept conspiracy theories as fact. The negative emotions one experiences during a crisis can cause the unconscious drive to construct order out of the chaos. In addition to overt emotional concerns such as anxiety, covert drives protect the body. Therefore, despite a conspiracy being wildly inaccurate and scientifically impossible, it may reach popular media sources and impact widespread society.

Unorthodox reasoning is accepted as fact when the mind desperately attempts to make sense of the disorder. At the same time, the rise of the internet has connected us with nearly inescapable access to information that conveniently provides several interpretations of the truth—individuals who are attracted to conspiracy information share similar interests and inherent qualities. Douglas & Robbie (2011) reveal that the relationship between a person's moral qualities and beliefs in conspiracy theories is highly mediated by projecting those qualities onto others. Machiavellianism is the personality trait conveying one's level of manipulativeness and is an indicator of a person's moral tendencies. Thus, machiavellian people will likely follow a movement when they experience a sense of community and belonging. Subsequently, these individuals often participate in a close-minded community with similar values. The values held by conspiracy theory communities are not often directed at positive global social change. For example, machiavellian individuals were more likely to believe government agents staged the 9/11 attacks because they were more likely to perceive that they would do so themselves if they were in the government's position (p. 7).

The article "Communicating to the Public in the Era of Conspiracy Theory" illustrates the ease at which conspiracy theories spread. More importantly, the inability of the government to communicate with the public during times of crisis is a particular concern to social scientists (2019). Connolly et al. (2019) explain that the lack of communication gatekeeping can create public confusion. Conspiracy theories about the Zika virus in the United States spread throughout social media. With 20% of Americans consider various conspiracy theories more reliable than authoritative sources (p.471). Online misinformation can spread quickly and is particularly harmful when governing bodies are working to manage an impending crisis. Connolly et al. (2019) highlight that government transparency, less political jargon, and social media can challenge the spread of conspiracy theories. A core concern with the rise in conspiracies is the tendency to contradict legitimate sources of information attempting to spread awareness about a potentially catastrophic situation. Not only do conspiracies contradict the information spread by the ruling bodies, they question the accuracy of scientific findings and challenge good intentions. The ongoing narrative dominant in conspiracy thinking is an extreme distrust of the government and ruling bodies. An anti-conformity narrative can be particularly harmful in cases where government support is required to protect the population.

Online conspiracy groups and cults have a similar influence on the individual. Dr. Janja Lalich is a sociologist and former member of a left-wing cult specializing in online conspiracy communities and cult dynamics. Lalich (2021) explains in an interview for Wired.com that online conspiracy groups demonstrate cult-like characteristics. Further, online communities offer similar feelings of belonging and fulfillment offered by cults. Moreover, people who believe in conspiracies have a recognizable pattern of behaviour. Lalich's framework on cults outlines four behaviours of a cult. The first of the four behaviours of a cult is that they typically have a transcendent belief system. A transcendent belief system is an overarching ideology that provides all the answers to the universe. Such as a unique place in the world or reason for existence. Thus, a cult is not necessarily religious. Instead, the group shares opinions and ideas about the meaning of life and social structures.

Typically, but not consistently, the cult belief system is enforced by a charismatic leader. Lalich (2021) argues individuals may take on the identity of the cult leader. Particularly morality or immorality as part of the resocialization process. Resocialization occurs when a group attempts to alter the sense of morality before joining the group. Cult members are expected to change their appearance, social connections and environment during resocialization. Cults and online conspiracy communities do not share the same intake process, and the communities project similar expectations. Both communities expect absolute willingness to participate in the cause. Most notable are control, influence and power distribution in conspiracy communities and cults. Leaders of the online conspiracy theory are much more likely to remain anonymous.

CHAPTER 9: INFLUENCE, CULTS, AND CONSPIRACIES

Further, it is likely that multiple people play the role on various occasions (wired, 2021).

Individuals who conform to a conspiratorial belief or join a cult community will experience a decline in positive relationships and overall safety. If the belief is in regards to medical science, individuals may avoid treatment, vaccinations or any form of healthcare for fear of exposure to illness. Del Vicario et al. (2016) emphasize that "scientific information., and their data, methods, and outcomes are readily identifiable and available. The origins of conspiracy theories are often unknown, and their content is strongly disengaged from mainstream society and sharply divergent from recommended practices." A particularly notable case is the conspiracy that childhood vaccinations would lead to autism in infants and children. This conspiracy is detrimental to individual health and gives rise to illnesses such as polio, which is nearly obsolete in regions where vaccination is a social expectation. Skepticism before the introduction of vaccinations is expected, but social expectations can be smashed once a socially influential individual or group decides to take action.

Another shared behaviour among cult and conspiracy communities is the prevalence of the concept of cognitive dissonance (Lalich, 2021). Cognitive dissonance is a cognitive process in which the brain can not process challenges to the belief system. Therefore results in the mind creating alternate explanations for the prevailing phenomena. Individuals are expected to stick with their long-standing belief systems when faced with information that challenges internal norms. However, some will pivot their perceptions to ease the cognitive dissonance. By pivoting, individuals open themselves to explanations originating from the conspiracy.

Moreover, if an individual experiences a dramatic social or environmental change, whether through moving or losing critical social connections, participating in a like-minded community can help reduce the pain caused by the loss. Sternisko et al. (2020) posit that context and motivational states influence one's perception of a conspiracy. Further, an individual's willingness to participate in the conspiracy community is heavily influenced by the person attempting to encourage participation. In other words, persuasion is an element in acquiring new members of an online conspiracy community. Though, the influence of online conspiracy communities is subtle. Rather than overt displays of power as demonstrated by arrogant cult leaders, people who conform to conspiracy theories believe the information is secret, consequential and special. Sternisko et al. (2020) explain that a shared sense of uniqueness characterizes online conspiracy theory communities. Participants tend to perceive the knowledge they hold as fact because the content will reinforce and legitimize their beliefs and values.

While a conspiracy theory can be true, like the Watergate scandal, most lack logic or scientific foundations. That being said, political and health conspiracies appear the most prevalent. Still, there are various forms of conspiracy, with many aimed at discrediting scientists and cultural groups. Van Prooijen and Douglas (2017) explain that the Jewish population is a frequent target of conspiratorial thinking, with the theory suggesting a Jewish plot to take over the world (p. 326). The Jewish conspiracy can be traced back to Medieval times when society blamed European Jewish peoples for the plague and failures during the Crusades. However, the conspiracy was fuelled by the first world war and the anti-Semitic spewing of Hitler, who blamed the Jewish people for his military failings. At the same time, Stalin blamed Jewish people for Naziesm in general, which is a stunning representation of victim blaming (p.326). Particularly in the case of celebrities' involvement in conspiracies, we see a mass acceptance movement, as was the case with the infamous Donald Trump brazenly sharing dangerous propaganda denying climate change and accusing Barack Obama of being born outside the United States (van Prooijen & Douglas, 2018). In this case, we see a prolific celebrity and business leader taking control of a narrative. Whether intentionally or not, the actions of well-known individuals created widespread conspiracy, particularly in online communities. Nevertheless, the case can be made that wealth and status allow the creation of conspiracy-filled propaganda for personal gain. It is evident the social, economic and political

126

elite employ false information and twist narratives to conform to personal and political objectives.

With the rise of misinformation and conspiracy theories, there are concerns from world leaders over how to communicate legitimate information about critical world events. Conspiracy theories have dangerous consequences for public health and social norms (Connolly et al., 2019). With the rise of online conspiracy theories, individuals are no longer required to interact with people in their immediate surroundings. Instead, online communities provide unlimited options for individuals to interact with like-minded individuals otherwise unavailable in their surrounding community.

In other words, technology allows for sharing of dubious information (p. 470). Specifically, internet conspiracy theories can spread like wildfire, which is extremely dangerous when faced with a crisis. Research conducted by Rothmund et al. (2022) on the pandemic denial of the German public found common behaviours among those who disagree with the scientific experts. A closer look at the traits shared amongst those who appear to be easily persuaded by conspiracy theories found distinct patterns of behaviour shared by people suspicious of scientific resources. Suspicion of powerful institutions and "mainstream" information is typical of those who participate in online conspiracy theories and cult groups. To assess the inherent qualities of science deniers, Rothmund et al. (2022) organized German research participants (n=1,575), from which two denial groups emerged. Dismissive participants made up 8% of the sample and displayed low-risk assessment, low compliance with containment measures and mistrust of politics. At the same time, 19% of participants made up the doubtful category. Doubtful participants were characterized by low cognitive reflection, high uncertainty in distinguishing between true and false claims and high social media intake. .0Risk assessment is the ability to comprehend the information and the potential harm. Thus risk assessment is influenced by the ability to understand the scientific evidence. Moreover, risk assessment is influenced by one's personal values and motivations. Therefore, Rothmund et al. (2022) findings suggest that individuals who are dismissive of information communicated by scientific experts are motivated by a lack of understanding.

To absorb novel information, the mind must be open and capable. Those who conform to conspiracy have a mindset of superiority and understanding, limited cognitive processing power, and critical thinking skills (Rothmund et al., 2022). Such a population can not comprehend that social movements will challenge their existing social norms and influence social change.

Further, people are easily persuaded by a narrative that aligns with values they may already hold. Subsequently, Del Vicario et al. (2016) found that people who read science news and conspiracy theories show similar consumption patterns concerning the content, the way each group interacts and shares the news and theory. Specifically, science news is usually "assimilated." In other words, it spreads quickly to more people. Further, the longer the information is available, the less interest it gains among society. In contrast, there is a positive correlation between the lifetime of a conspiracy theory and the number of believers, with the theory spreading slowly. Individuals may experience support in an online conspiracy community for an opinion they may not share with physical contacts. Such individuals may turn to conspiracy theories as an uncomplicated explanation for objectively complex human experiences. While making order out of chaos is human nature, searching for a solution that is the easiest to understand is dangerous, as not everyone has the same capacity for scientific knowledge. Social movements are fuelled by ignorance, mainly when the foundation is in a conspiracy.

Notably, the research conducted by Rothmund et al. (2022) found that individuals who show a high degree of doubt when faced with scientific information also have lower levels of higher education and cognitive reflection. In other words, people who struggle to believe scientific sources are less educated. Education allows for the ability to comprehend complex explanations for a phenomnea. Moreover, individuals with a low level of cognitive reflection struggle to think about the information they absorb simply. Then, it is likely that by engaging with scientific information, these individuals are experiencing cognitive dissonance. With this in mind, findings to show the experience of cognitive dissonance are particularly relevant in conspiracy theory and persuasion. Suppose the persuasive message appears to be beyond one's frame of understanding. In that case, it will make sense to turn to a more straightforward explanation, particularly if the simple explanation aligns with pre-existing values shared with a community of anonymous individuals on the internet. In general, Rothmund et al. (2022) findings suggest individual science deniers are motivated by diverse psychological processes. In other words, there appears to be a small group of self-confident and politically motivated people who dismiss the risk. The second, larger group requires simple answers and tends to perceive information from social media as accurate. The levels of cognitive processes are interesting as individuals with limited processing power are typically perceived as more easily influenced. It is apparent that cognitive capacity has a significant role to play in the ability to avoid conspiratorial thinking.

With the rise of disinformation, online digital information has become a concern of political and health care organizations as it is recorded as one of the main threats to human society (Del Vicario et al., 2016). Nevertheless, the media influences all facets of human life. A core concern is how people turn to media sources and how the news item will impact the viewers' belief systems and understanding of social norms. The nature of the media is to persuade viewers. Therefore, understanding the way persuasive messages are shared in conspiracy communities is essential to addressing the dangerous influences of media disinformation. Del Vicario et al. (2016) explain that most internet users share content that conforms to a single narrative. In other words, modern media has created an echo chamber where users share an idea, and the algorithm will continue to show related media items. Information is shared between friends and does not expand outside the echo chamber. This is why a conspiracy may spread slowly; the ideas are not spread on a massive scale. Instead, they are passed between like-minded individuals.

The echo chamber is particularly dangerous if the message is harmful. Conspiracy theory often includes holding an outside group accountable for pressing on the rights and freedoms of the participants. Nevertheless, due to exposure to conspiracy theories, individuals do not perceive themselves to change (Douglas & Sutton, 2008, p. 213). Instead, individuals exposed to persuasive media do not see themselves as impacted by the message. As Douglas & Sutton (2008) identified, individuals, underestimate the degree to which persuasive media influence them. This is defined as the third-person effect, which is the tendency for people to believe a persuasive media will not impact them the same way it does others. Hence, individuals who access conspiratory media do not believe themselves to be impacted. Seldom will people willingly admit they are gullible, particularly those who experience the sense of superiority that comes from accessing conspiratory information. Arguably, if the information one is accessing is framed as secret, unique and powerful, in addition to being persuasive, there is no space for the viewer to consider the information untrue.

Individuals who join online conspiracy theories by accessing information within an echo chamber are less likely to consider themselves impacted by persuasion. It can be seen that the message does not necessarily need to be persuasive. It can be argued conspiracy, and cult narratives are not inherently persuasive. Government and social institutions must persuade the public to avoid propaganda and conspiracy news. However, the internet is vast and nearly impossible to monitor. Then again, ruling institutions would be best suited to encourage individuals to ask questions and accept confusion as a temporary state. It has been shown that conspiracy and cult narratives do not hold inherent influence. Rather personal mental processing and social environment will set the stage for participation in a belief system that can potentially harm oneself and society. Hence, powerful institutions must share facts with absolute transparency and encourage critical thinking in order to prevent the influence of deviant institutions and belief systems.

References

Sternisko, A., Cichocka, A., & Van Bavel, J. J. (2020). The dark side of social movements: social identity, non-conformity, and the lure of conspiracy theories. Current Opinion in Psychology, 35, 1–6. https://doi.org/10.1016/j.copsyc.2020.02.007

Connolly, J. M., Uscinski, J. E., Klofstad, C. A., & West, J. P. (2019). Communicating to the Public in the Era of Conspiracy Theory. Public Integrity, 21(5), 469–476. https://doi.org/10.1080/10999922.2019.1603045

Douglas, Karen and Sutton, Robbie M. (2011) Does it take one to know one? Endorsement of conspiracy theories is influenced by personal willingness to conspire. British Journal of Social Psychology, 50 (3). pp. 544-552. ISSN 0144-6665.

Douglas, K. M., & Sutton, R. M. (2008). The hidden impact of conspiracy theories: Perceived and actual influence of theories surrounding the death of Princess Diana. The Journal of social psychology, 148(2), 210–221. https://doi.org/10.3200/SOCP.148.2.210-222

Jacobs, N. (1965). The phantom slasher of Taipei: Mass hysteria in a non-Western society. Social Problems, 12(3), 318-328.

Kirkpatrick, R. G. (1975). Collective consciousness and mass hysteria: collective behavior and anti-pornography crusades in Durkheimian perspective. Human Relations, 28(1), 63-84.

Rothmund, T., Farkhari, F., Ziemer, C. T., & Azevedo, F. (2022). Psychological underpinnings of pandemic denial-patterns of disagreement with scientific experts in the German public during the COVID-19 pandemic. Public Understanding of Science, 31(4), 437-457.

OED Online. (2022). common sense, n. and adj. Oxford University Press.

Lalich J. (2021). How Online Conspiracy Groups Compare to Cults. Wired. Wired.com van Prooijen, J.W., & Douglas, K. M. (2017). Conspiracy theories as part of history: The role of societal crisis situations. Memory

Studies, 10(3), 323–333. https://doi.org/10.1177/1750698017701615

van Prooijen, J. W., & Douglas, K. M. (2018). Belief in conspiracy theories: Basic principles of an emerging research domain. European journal of social psychology, 48(7), 897–908. https://doi.org/10.1002/ejsp.2530

CHAPTER 9: INFLUENCE, CULTS, AND CONSPIRACIES

Chapter 10: Conclusion

This book has so far taken an approach focused on reviewing the psychological concepts and practical applications of persuasion, power, and influence. However, it is also important to recognize and acknowledge that the practice of persuasion has ethical and philosophical dynamics that have been addressed for thousands of years.

From a philosophical perspective, it is notable that persuasion is a tool that can be used by individuals for both evil and good purposes as it can give effect to a lie as much as the truth. Famously, persuasion of the unethical kind is labelled as Machiavellian after the Italian renaissance statesman Niccolò Machiavelli. His book, The Prince, outlined the key persuasive characteristics of a ruler: being known as liberal, 'should desire to be held merciful and not cruel', leveraging and utilizing infamy, and to inspire fear or love (Kapust, 2010, p. 600). The objective of this book has been to offer readers tools and strategies in good faith for the purpose of promoting goodness and fairness.

The earliest philosophy concerning persuasion arises from a dialogue written by Plato in ancient Athens in 380 BC. In this Platonic dialogue, the characters Gorgias and Polus have a discussion about the ethics of rhetoric or persuasion. Plato communicates three messages within this story applicable to readers. First, Plato concludes that mastery of persuasive style and practical technique offers one more argumentative power than even a set of supportive facts or the truth. Plato indicates that perception is all that matters.

Second, Plato argues that persuasion merely involves a form of fakery in which to present an argument to appear stronger or weaker without imparting or addressing real knowledge. Plato suggests that the practice of persuasion has the potential to be hollow or unethical. Third, Plato, however, concludes that there are eternal versions of the truth that exist and that humanity can expect to obtain certain knowledge that itself can never be refuted and constitutes Truth in the sense of a noun and that can resist persuasion (Benoit, 1990, p. 256). Plato believes that for every persuasive message there is the capacity for the individual to exercise free choice through the application of rationality and the strategies that we have so far discussed within the book. Rhetorical teaching and learning extended well into the Roman Empire with speakers such as Cicero and Quintilian. Readers now join a long and distinguished line of thinkers and researchers which have focused their attention on how best to manage meaning and communicate with power and persuasion.

www.ingramcontent.com/pod-product-compliance
Lightning Source LLC
Chambersburg PA
CBHW030852270326
41928CB00008B/1335